Student Handbook to Sociology

Social Stratification and Inequality

Volume V

Student Handbook to Sociology

Social Stratification and Inequality

Volume V

LIZ GRAUERHOLZ

NICHOLAS A. GUITTAR

Facts On File
An Infobase Learning Company

Student Handbook to Sociology: Social Stratification and Inequality
Copyright © 2012 Liz Grauerholz and Nicholas A. Guittar

Facts On File, Inc.
An Imprint of Infobase Learning
132 West 31st Street
New York NY 10001

Library of Congress Cataloging-in-Publication Data

Student handbook to sociology / Liz Grauerholz, general editor.
    v. cm.
  Includes bibliographical references and index.
  Contents: v. 1. History and theory—v. 2. Research methods—v. 3. Social structure—v. 4. Socialization—v. 5. Stratification and inequality—v. 6. Deviance and crime—v. 7. Social change.
  ISBN 978-0-8160-8314-5 (alk. paper)—ISBN 978-0-8160-8315-2 (v. 1 : alk. paper)—ISBN 978-0-8160-8316-9 (v. 2 : alk. paper)—ISBN 978-0-8160-8317-6 (v. 3 : alk. paper)—ISBN 978-0-8160-8319-0 (v. 4 : alk. paper)—ISBN 978-0-8160-8320-6 (v. 5 : alk. paper)—ISBN 978-0-8160-8321-3 (v. 6 : alk. paper)—ISBN 978-0-8160-8322-0 (v. 7 : alk. paper)
  1. Sociology. I. Grauerholz, Elizabeth, 1958–
  HM585.S796 2012
  301—dc23   2011025983

Facts On File books are available at special discounts when purchased in bulk quantities for businesses, associations, institutions, or sales promotions. Please call our Special Sales Department at (212) 967-8800 or (800) 322-8755.

You can find Facts On File on the World Wide Web at
http://www.infobaselearning.com

Text design and composition by Erika K. Arroyo
Cover printed by Yurchak Printing, Landisville, Pa.
Book printed and bound by Yurchak Printing, Landisville, Pa.
Date Printed: April 2012
Printed in the United States of America

10 9 8 7 6 5 4 3 2 1

This book is printed on acid-free paper.

CONTENTS

FOREWORD

Social inequality is one of the most important topics within sociology, perhaps because it is so fundamental to understanding how societies are structured and because its effects are so profound. Although the concept of social inequality is abstract, its consequences are very real. Social inequality, a result of social stratification, affects how people live and creates circumstances that promote the likelihood of early death. Those who are privileged live longer, have access to affordable and quality health care, have more satisfying relationships, and enjoy a host of other benefits that elude those who are disadvantaged and have less.

To the best of our knowledge, all societies are characterized by the unequal treatment of certain groups. At the same time, societies are incredibly diverse and the types of inequalities and the degree to which they exist vary. For this reason, social inequality makes for a fascinating sociological study and raises interesting questions: What types of social inequalities persist in society? What are the social mechanisms that support systems of inequality? What are the effects on people—those at the top and those at the bottom? Are discrimination, prejudice, and oppression inevitable? Is it possible to eliminate social inequality?

As you'll learn in this volume, differences in how people are viewed, treated, and rewarded are often regarded as natural and normal. So unless you turn a critical eye onto these practices, you may never question why certain groups are treated differently—it's just the way things are and it's taken for granted. For instance, without a sociological perspective, you might simply assume that women are better parents and therefore naturally take on primary responsibility for raising children, or that children do not have the power to make responsible decisions for themselves, or that it's fine to "mass-produce" animals for our food and pleasure.

But sociology is about opening one's eyes to what is taken for granted. Thus, in this volume, you will explore in-depth several of the major ways in which human societies are stratified and the consequences for societies and its members. Ultimately, the question of what (if anything) we want to do about it becomes both a personal and societal issue. I hope this volume will bring you a little closer to making informed decisions about these important issues.

—Liz Grauerholz, University of Central Florida

INTRODUCTION

All societies have some system for stratifying groups, but this does not mean that stratification looks the same throughout cultures and societies. A sociological perspective on stratification leads us to explore the ways in which societies are stratified—that is, what criteria are used to differentiate groups from one another and most importantly, what are the consequences of stratification? Indeed, if we have any hope of improving society and individuals' lives, we must understand the causes and consequences of stratification. That is what this volume offers. At the most basic level, you will learn that stratification is at the base of social inequality. And as you'll also learn from this volume, the consequences of stratification and inequalities are widespread and devastating.

Sociologists have traditionally focused on inequality stemming from gender, social class, and race, and we focus much of our attention in this volume on these three forms of social inequality. Although these are the most widely studied and predominant forms of inequality in the United States, there are many other ways in which inequality permeates our lives and culture. In this volume, we expand our focus to include other types of social inequality that are not often found in textbooks on inequality. We make the argument here that children and animals are among the most oppressed groups in society, and to neglect examining their relationship to the larger social structure is to limit our understanding of society and how we live.

Our focus is primarily upon stratification systems and practices within the United States. But as the world becomes increasingly globalized, or interconnected, we begin to see how stratification is never isolated within one culture. Rather, stratification and inequalities are universal phenomena and very much linked. Practices within one country have implications for individuals' well-being across the world. To limit our perspective to just one group, especially such a powerful society as the United States, would be to ignore the many ways in which cultures can and do affect others.

We conclude with a discussion of what has been done, what is being done, and what might be done to reduce the devastating effects of social inequality. Armed with the information presented in this volume, you will be better informed about the problems that stem from stratification and inequality, as well as about successful endeavors to ameliorate or even prevent those effects. With that knowledge, you will be in a better position to affect changes you hope to see in the world. Ultimately, the future is in your hands and will be shaped by the decisions, choices, and strategies you use to deal with the problems you confront throughout your life.

CHAPTER 1

UNDERSTANDING STRATIFICATION AND INEQUALITY

Stratification refers to the division of society according to certain social categories such as age, race, class, or gender. All societies have some system for stratifying groups, although they differ in terms of what criteria are used. India, for example, has traditionally operated under a **caste system**, with heredity determining a person's ranking in society. Once born into a social caste, you remain there for the rest of your life. In other countries, skin color might be the distinguishing factor. Although the criteria used to stratify groups differ from society to society, once a system is established it serves as a basis for treating groups differently. In most cases, it promotes inequality and unfairness. The consequences of such systemic stratification have profound social implications, which we'll explore throughout this volume.

SOCIOLOGICAL PERSPECTIVES ON INEQUALITY

Sociologists generally study social inequality through the lens of stratification because stratification is the system through which inequality is reproduced or perpetuated within society. Although sociologists generally focus on three major forms of stratification—race, social class, gender—there are many ways in which societies are stratified. For instance, we also differentiate people on the basis of age, sexual orientation, religion, physical attractiveness, physical abilities, marital status, nationality, and even species.

An important key to understanding inequality from a sociological perspective is to know that *recognizing* difference is not the problem. What matters to sociologists is what these differences lead to. For example, gender stratification and inequality would not be of interest or concern to sociologists and feminist scholars if women were simply seen as different from men (e.g., capable of bearing children) but treated the same as men—that is, if they were paid the same wages, were at no greater risk of being sexually assaulted, were not viewed as the "weaker" sex, or objectified in media. The fact that all of these things affect women in negative ways is what makes the differences interesting to sociologists.

The example of gender differences illustrates another important point, the fact that differences and inequality are **social constructions** and are both created by and for the benefit of certain groups in society. You might at this point

Caste System

For many centuries, the caste system in India has used heredity as a basis for stratifying groups. If you were born into a family of Kshatriyas or Brahmins, you would enjoy considerable privilege, wealth, and respect throughout your life, regardless of whether you did any meaningful work. If, on the other hand, you were born into a family of *outcasts* (those literally outside of the caste system),

(above) **Group of Rajput Kshatriya men.** *(Wikipedia)*; *(next page)* **Dalit man walks down the street in Jaipur, India** *(Wikipedia. Photo by Thomas Schoch)*

be thinking "of course men and women are different—it's *obvious!*" And it is certainly true that there are a few visible (but mostly not so visible) biological differences between males and females. But in the grand scheme of things, these biological differences are quite inconsequential and really only come into play during pregnancy/childbirth and lactation, processes that occupy only a small percentage of women's lives (and for some women, none at all). Yet the *consequences* and the *meanings* we attach to perceived sex differences are enormous. Most sociologists would argue that there is nothing, or at least very little, in our *nature* that dictates that women take care of the home or that men are sexual aggressors. Thus, to understand why social inequality exists, we must move

you would be regarded as one of the "untouchables" (also known as Dalits) and would be forced to do the worst jobs for little reward. Although the caste system in India still exists, there have been government efforts to aid those individuals within the lower castes and Dalits.

away from biological explanations and explore the social forces that have given rise to stratification and inequality, and that means studying about differences and inequality as social constructions.

KEY CONCEPTS RELATED TO SOCIAL INEQUALITY
Social Stratification

Within any given society, individuals belong to various groups. For instance, you belong to a race group (e.g., Asian American), a social class (upper, middle, working, or lower), a species (human), a sex (male or female), and an age group (e.g., young, middle, old); you also have a sexual preference (e.g., heterosexual) and other distinguishing characteristics (e.g., level of education or marital status) that make you part of some subgroup of your society. Stratification may be centered on physical characteristics with which you are born and over which you have little ability to change (race, sex, height, eye color, etc.). These are referred to as **ascribed characteristics**. Stratification can also be based on **achieved characteristics** which are acquired or earned. Examples include marital status, education, and occupation.

The difference between ascribed and achieved statuses is not always clear. Certain characteristics that seem to be inherently *ascribed* may be altered throughout life, resulting in a newly *achieved* characteristic. For example, you may be ascribed the status of *male* at birth but achieve the status of *female* if you undergo medical treatment or simply "pass" with dress and mannerisms. Some would argue that you may be born gay or lesbian (this is a hotly debated topic, of course) but still live a heterosexual lifestyle and hence achieve heterosexual status by dating and marrying someone of the other sex, parenting a child, and so on. Some traits such as attractiveness may be genetically inherited and thought to be ascribed, but attractiveness can and is often manipulated (through dress, makeup, plastic surgery) and is therefore achieved.

Not all societies recognize the same groups or stratify people the same way. For example, age is a stratification criterion recognized and emphasized in several societies. One society, however, might place very strong emphasis on age in a way that holds older people in high esteem, regardless of religion or gender or other variables. But another society that emphasizes the same criterion may interpret it differently: Whereas one culture might revere older people, another might be more youth-oriented and therefore consider being old undesirable.

If you've taken a geology course, you've learned that there are strata or layers of rock that can be distinguished from other layers and that these are vertically layered. Social strata can be thought of in a similar way. The strata in each social category are figuratively ranked one above the other, in what is known as a **hierarchy**. For instance, social class is stratified from upper-class (the rich) to lower-class (the poor). Social class is probably the easiest to recognize as being stratified, but stratification in other social groupings are also rather obvious. For

Societies assign status by criteria, but the criteria are not always viewed the same way. In some cultures, the woman at the left would be considered far more powerful than the woman at the right. In a youth-oriented culture, however, women lose power and status as they age. *(Wikimedia)*

instance, it does not take much digging to see that men occupy higher positions than women, that heterosexuals enjoy more rights and higher status than gay and lesbian persons, and that American citizens within the United States have a higher standard of living than persons from many other nations. Of course, there may be individual women who are more powerful than individual men or individual gay men who have more status in society than individual straight men. But *as a group*, women, gay and lesbian persons, immigrants, and so on occupy lower positions within the stratification system.

Quite often, various stratification systems are embedded within larger systems of stratification. For instance, within the upper-class strata, being "old rich" (having inherited money) is better than being "nouveau riche" ("new rich" or having acquired wealth recently). In the United States, members of a racial minority often view being light-skinned as more desirable than being darker-skinned. Such values are derived from the larger social structure (which values being white over other races), but it can also be seen as a system within a larger system that further differentiates and stratifies groups. We can also move beyond a particular group, culture, or country and observe stratification and inequality on a larger, more global scale. For instance, so-called developed countries (such as the United States or Great Britain) possess considerably more influence and power than developing or underdeveloped countries (such as Poland or Haiti).

Where you fall within any given stratification system (whether it be gender, race, social class, age, etc.) will in large part determine access to resources in society (money, services, opportunity, etc.). Those people found in the higher strata for each category have far greater access to resources than those further down. For instance, compared to members of the lower class, those in the upper class have greater income and savings (money), access to better health care and schooling (services), and personal connections to other wealthy people (opportunity). These forms of **capital**, as sociologists refer to them, are both causes and consequences of social inequality: The more you have, the more you get; and the more you get, the more you have.

Privilege

At the heart of inequality and any stratification system is the notion of privilege. Those within the upper strata are afforded certain privileges or advantages by virtue of being in that group. Although some of these benefits are earned through effort and hard work (e.g., you study really hard, earn excellent grades, and are granted the privilege to enroll in honors-level or advanced placement courses), many forms of privilege in society are based upon ascribed characteristics or circumstances into which you are born (e.g., race, family position). Thus, **privilege** could be seen as an *unearned advantage that some experience regardless of merit or achievement*. This idea was wonderfully illustrated by Peggy McIntosh in her essay "Unpacking the Invisible Knapsack," which explores *white privilege*. As McIntosh observes, white privilege is "an invisible package of unearned assets, which I can count on cashing in each day. . . . [It] is like an invisible weightless knapsack of special provisions, maps, passports, code books, visas, clothes, tools, and blank checks."

Expressing a similar point of view, sociologist Michael Kimmel uses the analogy of running with or against the wind to illustrate the influence of privilege. Those who hold some sort of privilege are running *with* the wind at their backs (they don't see it, but it's there), while those without privilege are running *into* the wind (with the wind as an invisible yet obvious hindrance). The same amount of effort has markedly different outcomes depending on your vantage point. Our discussions of privilege and its relationship to inequality throughout this book is an attempt to "make the wind visible" so that we can better understand how social inequality operates.

Intersectionality

Thinking about privilege can also help us see ways in which we may be both advantaged and disadvantaged. Groups often get lumped together (all women, all blacks, all rich people, etc.), but we should avoid thinking in such monolithic terms because statuses *intersect* with one another to produce multiple layers of stratification and experiences with oppression. Thus, two women may have completely different experiences with stratification depending upon their social class, race, nationality, and so on. These multiple systems of stratification inter-sect with one another to produce complex social realities. We may be privileged in some ways but disadvantaged in other ways. If you are a white female in the United States, for instance, you will have a social advantage over some people (e.g., black women) but not over others (e.g., white men).

In fact, although it may be difficult to see at times, everyone reading this book is privileged in some way and most likely not in other ways. A co-worker related a story about a class he was teaching in which he was explaining these concepts of privilege and oppression. One of his students—who was African American and lesbian—stated that she found it difficult to understand how she could possibly be considered privileged, given her race, sexual orientation, and gender. A male student, who was blind, remarked that she could at least

In what ways might each of these individuals be privileged? In what ways are they likely to be disadvantaged? Sociologists are not interested so much in whether or which one of these individuals is more oppressed than the others, but in the ways in which various forms of privilege intersect with one another. *(Shutterstock)*

navigate her way around her neighborhood and the university without assistance. Indeed, an interesting thing about privilege is how generally unrecognized it is to those who hold it. Peggy McIntosh claims that we are meant to remain oblivious to it. In this way, we can continue believing that whatever wealth and status we possess is due to our own hard work and talents, rather than the product of larger social forces.

Oppression

Although the word "**oppression**" may seem extreme, it does capture the experience of some groups or individuals in society who feel weighted down by social inequality. To be oppressed, according to the Merriam-Webster dictionary, suggests that one is subject to extreme exercises of authority or power (e.g., violence) and feels weighed down (or *pressed*) by these forces. One or a few blocked opportunities or experiences with discrimination will not lead to feeling oppressed; instead, oppression is a feeling borne from a lifetime of discrimination and prejudice. It means that you have internalized the idea that trying to break out of your life circumstances would be futile.

Like privilege, oppression is often very difficult to recognize. One of the best metaphors for thinking about oppression and why it is difficult to see comes from Marilyn Frye's *The Politics of Reality*, where she describes gender oppression as a *birdcage*:

> If you look very closely at just one wire in the cage, you cannot see the other wires. If your conception of what is before you is determined by this myopic focus, you could look at that one wire, up and down the length of it, and be unable to see why a bird would not just fly around the wire any time it wanted to go somewhere. Furthermore, even if, one day at a time, you myopically inspected each wire, you still could not see why a bird would have trouble going past the wires to get anywhere. There is no physical property of any one wire, nothing that the closest scrutiny could discover, that will reveal how a bird could be inhibited or harmed by it except in the most accidental way. It is only when you step back, stop looking at the wires one by one, microscopically, and take a macroscopic view of the whole cage, that you can see why the bird does not go anywhere; and then you will see it in a moment. It will require no great subtlety of mental powers. It is perfectly obvious that the bird is surrounded by a network of systematically related barriers, no one of which would be the least hindrance to its flight, but which, by their relations to each other, are as confining as the solid walls of a dungeon.

Thus, to be oppressed is to be surrounded by a network of barriers and pressures that shape all aspects of one's life. In some cases, oppressed groups are *literally* caged or physically constrained, as in the case of animals (see Chapter 5) or human slaves (see Chapter 2). More often, sociologists who talk about oppression are referring to how individuals' lives can become so constrained, through laws or norms or violence, that the option to just leave or improve their circumstances is too difficult or even unthinkable.

HOW IS INEQUALITY REPRODUCED?

Social inequality is **systemic**. It is built into the very fabric of society—its norms, institutions, values, laws, and so on. Sociologists, therefore, focus on various ways in which people and societies perpetuate social inequality, ranging from the institutional to the individual.

Institutionalized Inequality

Institutional discrimination is the term used to describe unequal practices and treatment of groups within social institutions (education, housing, economy, etc.). For example, organizations may have policies or governments may have laws that legitimate treating socially defined groups of people differently, regardless of their individual abilities. As recently as the 1970s many companies banned women from working certain types of jobs because women were thought to be physically unfit for such jobs. In the early 20th century, when working women married, they were no longer allowed to work outside the home. A contemporary example of institutionalized inequality or discrimination are laws prohibiting gays and lesbians from marrying in most states.

Whenever institutionalized discrimination exists, there will be cultural attitudes that support these practices. For example, when blacks and women were prohibited from voting earlier in our country's history, it was assumed that they were incapable of making intelligent decisions. Such cultural attitudes and beliefs, even if they are based on falsehoods and overgeneralizations, are necessary to keep a system of inequality in place.

Cultural Ideology

Social inequality is supported and legitimated by **cultural ideology**, or beliefs about the rightness of certain cultural practices. Ideology allows us to justify a system or practice, no matter how illogical or immoral it may be. For instance, slavery existed in the United States because dark-skinned Africans were viewed as subhuman. Even Thomas Jefferson, who declared that "We hold these truths to be self evident, that *all men are created equal*," owned slaves until his death in 1826.

Meritocracy refers to the belief that personal and professional successes are based on achievement and merit earned through hard work alone. In capitalist societies like the United States, the ideology of meritocracy serves to justify the enormous differences in wealth found throughout society. Within the parameters of this ideology, it is theoretically possible for an individual born into poverty in rural Mississippi to become one of the richest, most powerful women on the planet (as Oprah Winfrey did) but it is highly unlikely. But ideology does not have to match reality. It just has to be accepted so that it helps to perpetuate systems of inequality.

Individual Beliefs and Practices

Social inequality could not persist if it were not supported and perpetuated by individuals in everyday interactions—on the street, in organizations, in the family, and so on. Individual beliefs and actions—including prejudice, discrimination, "othering," and stereotyping—play an important role in reproducing social inequality.

Prejudice is a *prejudgment* about something or someone, and usually refers to an unfavorable opinion or feeling toward that something or someone. It can be relatively minor and inconsequential, such as detesting the Red Sox if you're a Yankees fan, or more serious, such as believing that immigrants are dirty, women are too emotional, or poor people are lazy. Prejudice is a key part of reproducing social inequality because such beliefs, when unexamined, can justify bad treatment. If you believe poor people are just lazy, then you are unlikely to support government interventions to help the poor. Or if you believe women are very emotional, then you aren't likely to vote for a woman presidential candidate or appoint a woman as CEO of a major organization.

Such perceptions of different groups are often rooted in stereotypes. A **stereotype** is an exaggerated and often oversimplified belief associated with a particular group of people. Examples of stereotypes are that jocks are dumb, people from the South are "slow," and women are poor drivers. Stereotypical thinking allows us to ignore contrary information about individuals (the highly intelligent "jock" becomes the *exception*) and does not force us to reconsider unfair systems or practice. In this way, stereotypes help to reinforce social inequalities.

The concepts of prejudice and stereotyping capture our thinking and feelings, but individuals don't necessarily *act* on these feelings. **Discrimination**, on the other hand, is actual overt behavior that results in the unfair treatment of a person or group on the basis of group membership. Discrimination exists when a teacher does not call on boys in the classroom, or a used-car salesperson offers his male customers better deals than he offers women, or an employer routinely hires only attractive applicants. Although many types of blatant discrimination are illegal, it still occurs in more subtle ways and in everyday interactions.

Prejudice and discrimination often work hand-in-hand, but not always. In his 1968 book *Social Theory and Social Structure*, Robert Merton discussed how prejudice and discrimination can be consistent, for example, when persons are both unprejudiced and nondiscriminatory (what he called **all-weather liberals**) or prejudiced and discriminatory (**all-weather bigots**). Here, attitudes and behaviors are consistent. Sometimes, however, our attitudes and behavior are

The Relationship Between Prejudice and Discrimination

	Does Not Discriminate	Does Discriminate
Unprejudiced	Unprejudiced nondiscriminator (all-weather liberal)	Unprejudiced discriminator (fair-weather liberal)
Prejudiced	Prejudiced nondiscriminator (timid bigot)	Prejudiced discriminator (all-weather bigot)

Source: Robert Merton, *Social Theory and Social Structure*, 1968.

not consistent. Such is the case with those who are prejudiced but do not discriminate (**timid bigots**) and those who are unprejudiced but do discriminate (**fair-weather liberals**). An example of a timid bigot is the retail manager who is convinced that African Americans are inferior employees, but who still treats blacks and whites the same on the job. An example of a fair-weather liberal is the football coach who believes that members of all races are equal in ability but places only white players in the quarterback position. This last example brings up an important point that is frequently overlooked: Intent is *not* a prerequisite for discrimination. In other words, not all harm is caused by people who are obvious bigots. Although you may believe in total equality, your actions can still unintentionally discriminate against certain populations.

The oppression of any group, whether it be women or Native Americans or immigrants, involves **othering**, something that occurs when those individuals in power are perceived as the "normal" and desirable group, and individuals who do not fall within that group are perceived as different, "less than," and inferior. Consider, for example, how race is sometimes designated "whites" and "nonwhites." Whites are clearly the reference group—that group to which all others are compared (and evaluated). No matter that the group "nonwhites" includes tremendous diversity—they simply become the "other."

Some sociologists argue that othering is critical in reproducing inequality. By definition, the "other" is not "normal." It is easier to exploit or abuse those who are different, and to justify poor treatment or discrimination of these individuals. For instance, beliefs about the "inherent" weakness of women or "natural" intelligence of certain races provide justification for not hiring women or minorities in certain types of jobs.

SUMMARY
Social inequality has occupied a central place in sociology for decades. Traditionally, sociologists focused on three main forms of inequality and strati-

fication—gender, race, and social class—but in recent years, researchers have expanded interest to other areas where inequality and stratification occurs. What we have learned is that certain common processes are at work to create systems of inequality and to maintain them, whether we're talking about stratification by gender, race, class, abilities, sexual orientation, religion, or nationality. These processes occur at the institutional, cultural, and individual levels. Thus, to understand how inequality is reproduced in society (and how to achieve greater social equality) one must examine it from multiple angles. It is not simply a matter of some people being prejudiced or lacking laws to remedy unfairness. These things contribute to the problem of inequality but are not sufficient to sustain it. As you'll see throughout this volume, social inequality is pervasive and perpetuated at all levels of social life.

Further Reading

Frye, Marilyn. *The Politics of Reality*. Trumansburg, New York: The Crossing Press, 1983.

Grusky, David B. *Social Stratification: Class, Race, and Gender in Sociological Perspective*. Boulder, Colo.: Westview Press, 2001.

Hill Collins, Patricia. *Black Feminist Thought: Knowledge, Consciousness, and the Politics of Empowerment*. New York: Routledge, 1999.

Massey, Douglas S. *Categorically Unequal: The American Stratification System*. New York: Russell Sage Foundation, 2007.

Merton, Robert King. 1968. *Social Theory and Social Structure*. New York, NY: Free Press.

Schwalbe, Michael. *Rigging the Game: How Inequality Is Reproduced in Everyday Life*. New York: Oxford University Press, 2008.

Tilly, Charles. *Durable Inequality*. Berkeley, CA.: University of California Press, 1999.

CHAPTER 2

ECONOMIC STRATIFICATION AND INEQUALITY

INTRODUCTION

From the time we are children, we learn about being rich or poor. We see visible signs of wealth and poverty virtually everywhere we look. Your best friend in elementary school had the coolest—and biggest selection of—toys, but the other friend you played with at school always wore the same clothes and never had new school supplies. Some friends got (nice!) cars from their parents for their birthdays; others rode the bus. On some level, you probably compared yourself to these other people—you knew you weren't as well off as Ellen or Josh, but you also knew you had it much better than David or Julia. Like most people, you might have questioned your own economic circumstances (*Why can't I have those things too?*), but you probably didn't question the economic system as a whole (*Is it fair that some people have so much and others so little?*). The economic arrangements that we experience growing up seemed natural and normal—some people simply had more than others, and you were either one of the lucky ones, or not.

One of the most important sociological insights into economic stratification is that all systems of stratification, including those based on economics, are social constructions. There are many ways in which economic resources can be distributed throughout society, but the systems with which we are most familiar—capitalism and social class—do not emerge naturally. They came about because of certain historical, cultural, and political forces. Furthermore, there is nothing inherently meaningful or superior about capitalism or social class systems, although we are usually taught otherwise. An economic structure, such as our social class structure, becomes meaningful only within social contexts. This implies that the meaning and definitions of social class vary within and depend on social, historical, and political contexts. In fact, you might be considered rich by one standard, and poor by another, even though your income and possessions remain the same.

In this chapter, we explore common economic systems of stratification, with particular focus on the open-class system, which operates in the United States and other Western societies. We examine how such systems embody economic inequality and the ways such inequality is maintained in society. Finally, we look at the consequences of economic inequality in people's lives.

ECONOMIC SYSTEMS OF STRATIFICATION

Economic stratification is a feature of all societies, although the structures that define a particular society can differ. Again, since stratification is a social construction, the forms it takes vary depending upon historical, political, and cultural factors. The major forms of economic stratification include systems based on caste, feudalism, slavery, and open class systems. Each of these is a complex system, with complex causes, and involves far more than just economic stratification. Each system is reinforced by institutional (commonly religious) and ideological practices.

In Chapter 1 we discussed the caste system, a social phenomenon still prevalent in India, in which heredity determines your ranking in society. Once you are born into a social caste, you remain there for the rest of your life. Your economic standing—whether you enjoy immense wealth or abject poverty—is determined by which family into which you were born. In Medieval Europe, a system called **feudalism** was in place. Feudal systems were like caste systems in that they were based on heredity—the family you were born into usually determined your economic situation. In feudal systems, large numbers of peasants, serfs, and laborers worked for and had to answer to a handful of aristocratic landowners. There was a strong division between these two groups of people. Both caste and feudal systems are propped up by religious ideologies that legitimate the structures and discourage dissent. The caste system is believed to have originated from the Vedas, or sacred Hindu texts, while the feudal system was based upon a religious doctrine known as the **Divine Right of Kings**, which maintained that monarchs derived their authority directly from God and therefore had the right to command others.

Slavery is another system of economic stratification, one that has figured prominently in numerous societies throughout history. There are references to slaves in the Old Testament, for example, and slaves played a major role in ancient Roman culture. We are all familiar with the institution of slavery in the United States prior to the Civil War, a time when millions of individuals of African descent were considered the property of wealthy white men and, as such, could be bought and sold. But slavery is not just a thing of the past. Modern-day slavery, now commonly referred to as **human trafficking,** involves the sale and transport of human beings for profit. Often, it is intertwined with **sexual slavery**—the practice of selling women (and even young girls and boys) for the purpose of prostitution. Human trafficking may also involve domestic, migrant, factory labor. We may think human trafficking takes place only in poor, developing countries, but it is shockingly common in the United States (see sidebar).

The system of economic stratification with which we are most familiar is the **open-class system**, which allows for **social mobility**—movement between classes—and therefore gives individuals the opportunity to improve their social standing. Another feature of open-class systems is the relative ease with which members of different social classes (middle class, upper class, etc.) may interact with one another. In the United States, for example, there are many groups whose membership crosses class boundaries. Examples of these are religious groups, political parties, civic organizations, and even social organizations, such as Little League Baseball. This sort of interclass mingling is virtually unheard of in fixed systems of stratification such as caste systems.

SOCIOLOGICAL PERSPECTIVES ON SOCIAL CLASS
Social class is the predominant stratification system in the United States and in many parts of the world. Sociological thinking about social class stems in part from the work of Karl Marx, who witnessed a growing disparity between two rival classes at the dawn of the Industrial Revolution in Europe. The upper class, or **bourgeoisie**, included an elite group of individuals who owned property, factories, and production processes. The workers, or **proletariat**, provided labor that enabled the bourgeoisie to enhance their wealth and power. Marx was concerned with the plight of the proletariat whose lives were deteriorating while the social elite continued to gain power and influence in society.

Max Weber, writing about 50 years after Marx, described the advent of the middle class, which comprised facility managers, small entrepreneurs, and other professionals who were economically better off than manual laborers but less privileged than the social elite. By this time, social class was no longer so evenly split between two rival classes. Rather, an emerging middle class was gaining power and prestige, and class structures in modern industrialized societies were shifting. Observing this phenomenon, Weber began to define social class in broader terms, namely what sociologists began to call **socioeconomic status**. Socioeconomic status includes not just income but prestige, power, and respect. For sociologists, socioeconomic status is typically measured by income, education, and occupational status.

It follows then that social class is a multidimensional concept that goes beyond income (how much money one earns). It also goes beyond **wealth**, which can be thought of as the accumulation of money or assets in excess of an individual's expenses (and thus, something that can be passed on to future generations). Social class also includes **prestige**, or the honor and esteem associated with holding a certain position or place within the social hierarchy. For instance, teachers are held in relatively high esteem despite the fact that they earn considerably less than many professionals who are held in lower esteem, say, lawyers or politicians. Some would also include **privilege**, or the advantage

Human Trafficking in the United States

Fruits and vegetables produced and sold in the United States are oftentimes very inexpensive. So what is behind these great deals we get at the checkout? What makes them possible? Consider for just a moment how much hard work it takes to get a single tomato from a grower's field to your refrigerator. Supermarkets around the country buy their produce from local and often not-so-local growers, and these growers rely on manual labor to harvest the products. What we seldom hear about is how growers utilize cheap labor to make a profit while still pleasing the supermarkets and consumers with low prices. The cheapest labor comes from exploited farm workers, most of whom are undocumented immigrant workers and some of whom are modern-day slaves.

The Coalition of Immokalee Workers (CIW), a community-based organization located in southwest Florida, fights for the rights of immigrants working in low-wage jobs in Florida. One of the groups that the CIW fights for is Florida's tomato farm workers. Why? For starters, some farms in Florida pay the pickers of their produce as little as 45 cents for a 32 pound bucket of tomatoes (or 1.4 cents per pound). This rate of pay has remained virtually unchanged over the past 30 years. Most workers have no benefits: no health insurance, no sick leave, no mandated breaks, and no voice. In extreme cases, workers even fall victim to slavery. In one case, a group of men were forced to work as involuntary servants (slaves) for two and a half years at a home in Immokalee, Florida.

These men were lured to the area with the promise of making a decent wage. When they arrived, a local man named Cesar Navarrete offered them room and board in exchange for a portion of their wages. One of the workers, Mariano Lucas Domingo, ended up living in the back of a container truck located in the backyard of the property with no running water, no toilet, and two roommates. Lucas figured his work would quickly pay off his debts, and he would then seek better work and better accommodations. Instead his debts magically kept growing, as Navarrete was confiscating and cashing Lucas's checks. If Lucas spoke up about his debt, challenged Navarrete, or missed a day of work, he would be beaten or locked inside a container truck. After 30 months of forced servi-

enjoyed by people who belong to certain social groups simply by virtue of their membership in those groups. Those with privilege, whether it stems from race, social class, sexual orientation, or gender, will have an easier time obtaining education, employment, health care, and numerous other social benefits that increase one's likelihood of achieving or maintaining a high class status.

Social class has profound impacts on everyone and serves to categorize, stereotype, and generalize others as well as ourselves. Americans typically recognize four basic social classes: upper, middle, working, and lower. Interestingly, there are no formal criteria to determine which classes exist or who belongs in

tude, Lucas was able to break free and escape. But this heartbreaking story is not unique; it is part of a growing trend. Men and women who are invisible members of society are the victims of modern-day slavery right here in our own backyards.

For more information about the Coalition of Immokalee Workers, go to http://www.ciw-online.org/about.html or http://www.gourmet.com/magazine/2000s/2009/03/politics-of-the-plate-the-price-of-tomatoes

For more information about human trafficking, go to the Federal Bureau of Investigation (FBI) Website (http://www.fbi.gov/about-us/investigate/civilrights/human_trafficking). The FBI tracks cases of human trafficking because it is linked to major criminal and drug cartels.

A migrant laborer in the tomato fields outside Immokalee, Florida. *(Photo by Scott Robertson)*

which group. The criteria are rather fluid—mostly because we tend to use different criteria when determining our own social class as well as that of others. Most people identify themselves as middle or working-class and avoid labeling themselves as upper or lower class—even those individuals who by almost anybody's standards would qualify for one of these extremes (e.g., they are in the top 5 percent of wage earners or they live below the official poverty line). Nonetheless, as sociologist Dennis Gilbert asserts, there is strong agreement about the relative *ranking* of social classes. That is, there is strong agreement that the upper class is ranked more highly than the middle, which in turn is higher than the working, and that the lower class ranking is indeed the lowest.

The Gap Between Upper and Lower

The gap between rich and poor in the United States is growing. That is, the rich are getting richer and the poor are getting poorer. In fact, the gap between rich and poor is wider than it has been at any time since 1928. Between 1979 and 2007, the average income of those in the wealthiest 1 percent of the population grew by 229 percent (compared to a modest 6 percent for those in the bottom 50 percent). In his work *Who Rules America?* G. William Domhoff noted that in 2006 the top 1 percent of households held 42.9 percent of the nation's financial wealth. Domhoff further noted that the top 20 percent of households represented 93 percent of the nation's financial wealth. Flip that statistic around

Social Class Positions

Class	Percent of Population	Annual Income	Occupations
Upper-upper class	1%	$2.0 Million	Investors, heirs, executives, owners of large businesses
Upper-middle class	14%	$150,000	Upper managers, professionals, owners of medium-sized businesses
Middle class	30%	$70,000	Lower management, foremen, semi-professionals, nonretail sales
Working class	30%	$40,000	Low-skill manual, clerical, retail sales
Working poor	13%	$25,000	Lowest-paid manual, retail, and service workers
Underclass	12%	$15,000	Menial jobs, part-time (under) employed, and unemployed

Source: Dennis Gilbert, *The American Class Structure in an Age of Growing Inequality*, 2011.

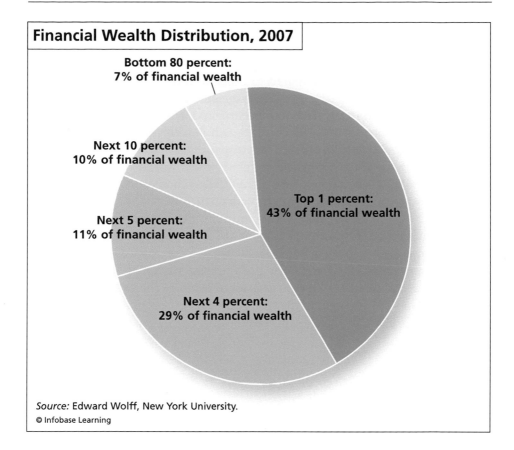

Financial Wealth Distribution, 2007

Bottom 80 percent:
7% of financial wealth

Next 10 percent:
10% of financial wealth

Top 1 percent:
43% of financial wealth

Next 5 percent:
11% of financial wealth

Next 4 percent:
29% of financial wealth

Source: Edward Wolff, New York University.
© Infobase Learning

and we find that 80 percent of Americans were competing for the remaining 7 percent of the country's wealth. In dollar terms, the wealth of the richest 1 percent of Americans totaled about 16.8 trillion dollars, which was $2 trillion more than the combined wealth of the lowest 90 percent of Americans.

It's nearly impossible for us to conceive of money in this way, or what the gap actually means in real dollars. One of the best ways to visualize this gap is to conceptualize it as an L-curve (for more information about the L-curve, and an interactive Web site, go to www.lcurve.org). Picture yourself in the middle (or median) of the income distribution in the United States—about half of all families earn less than you and about half earn more. Now imagine your income in terms of actual money. Your median family income (about $40,000) would be a stack of $100 bills about 1.6 inches high. The L-curve uses a football field to represent the income distribution in the United States, so you'd be in the middle (the median), or on the 50 yard line. Families at the 95 yard line (top 95 percent of U.S. families) have a stack of $100 bills about 4 inches high. At the 99 yard line, it's about a foot high. However, when you reach the very end, which represents the wealthiest individuals, the stack would extend into the strato-sphere—more than 5 times higher than Mt. Everest!

You might be wondering if the gap between rich and poor is better or worse in the United States compared to other countries. Timothy Smeeding, a renowned economist, compared the average income of those at the 90th per-centile (wealthy) to those at the 10th percentile (poor) of income for each of 30 nations. In the United States, those at the 90th percentile made 5.45 times as much as those at the 10th percentile. This disparity exceeds that of all the other comparably developed nations in the sample. In other words, the class structure in the United States is much more spread out (taller) than are class structures in other, comparable nations. For example, with an income ratio of 2.9, the income ratio in Finland was nearly half of that found in the United States (Finland's class structure is flatter—wealthy and poor are closer together in terms of their annual earnings).

The recent economic decline has not hurt the richest individuals in the United States but has been devastating for the poor. The 2010 U.S. Census showed that the 2009 incomes of the wealthiest five percent of Americans (those who earn over $180,000) actually increased, while the income of families earn-ing $50,000 or less dropped. This phenomenon has contributed to what is com-monly referred to as the shrinking of the middle class. Because the "middle class" comprises those who sustain the economy (through buying homes, cars, college educations, and various other consumer goods and services), there are major economic implications of this decline for society as a whole.

Social (Im)Mobility

Many people are not disturbed by such gross income inequalities because they assume that everyone can get ahead if they are willing to work hard enough. Others believe that they personally have a chance to make millions of dollars and therefore have a personal interest in seeing that the income distribution pattern in the United States does not change.

In reality, the chances of changing one's social class position within our open-class system are slim. Most people, if they do shift social classes, stay in roughly the same position, moving into a subcategory just above or just below their current social class (e.g., from middle class to upper-middle class). "Cin-derellas," who move from poverty to wealth, are extremely rare.

Even long-standing pathways from rags to riches have faded. Education, for example, has traditionally been the main source of social mobility, especially for the middle class. But a college education—the traditional pathway to a better life—has declined in value and holds less promise than it once did. This is due in part to the fact that a college-education has become the norm, not the excep-tion. In their book *The Race Between Education and Technology*, economists Lawrence Katz and Claudia Goldin note that in 1915, 75 percent of Americans had no more than an elementary school education; by the beginning of the 21st century, that percentage had dwindled (to 3 percent). Globalization and technological advances, which now allow employers to hire workers overseas for lower wages, also have contributed to the decline in the value of education in America.

An interesting corollary to the subject of social mobility is that most people often equate this concept with **upward mobility**—increasing one's social standing. But social mobility goes both ways, and individuals can easily move down the socioeconomic ladder, a process known as **downward mobility**. Downward mobility can be the result of job loss, divorce, demotion (as opposed to promotion) at the workplace, or widespread stock-market downturns, like the ones we've seen in recent years. It can also occur when people are cheated out of their retirement pensions or investments and are forced to start over or survive on much less than they had planned. Women are especially at risk for downward mobility when they get divorced. One reason is that women's wage-earning potential is likely to be less than their husbands'. In addition, they are more likely to retain custody of their children. Thus, after divorce, their wage-earning power and potential are lessened while their economic responsibilities to others remain the same or increase.

In the worst cases, downward mobility can lead to marginalized living conditions and even homelessness. Lack of affordable housing, job insecurity (including job loss), and unexpected expenses (e.g., medical bills) can devastate individuals and families. Among these, the disappearance of affordable housing may be especially critical. According to the National Alliance to End Homelessness, the cost of housing has risen faster than incomes. In fact, the organization claims that about 15 percent of Americans pay more than half their income on housing. This is a fact corroborated by the U.S. Census, which reports that 37 percent of Americans who have mortgages on their homes spend 30 percent or more of their household incomes on housing.

Here again, a personal perspective may make these facts and figures more meaningful. Think back to an earlier exercise where you stood in the middle of the football field with about $40,000 income. After taxes, you will have about $35,000. If you spend 30 percent of your gross income on housing, that leaves about $24,000 or $2000 per month. That may seem like a lot to a single person who is working while attending college, but apply this to a household and then consider that it must cover all other expenses—medical bills, car loans, insurance, food, utilities, gasoline, clothing, educational expenses, basic necessities, and any leisure activities. This leaves very little for savings. You can probably imagine how a major medical bill or legal expense could cause a family's position to plummet. And, of course, we're talking about median family income; for those families who fall below this level (that is, the half below median), the situation is far more precarious.

HOW IS SOCIAL CLASS INEQUALITY MAINTAINED?

In Chapter 1, we discussed myriad ways in which social inequality is perpetuated in society through institutional discrimination or cultural stereotyping. Here, we apply these processes to understanding how such inequality is maintained, with the underlying premise that practices at the individual, interpersonal, cultural, and institutional levels all contribute to social class inequality. Although we discuss processes and practices on each level separately, it should be noted that these are all interconnected and can operate at multiple levels. For instance, parenting styles (which can be thought of as an interpersonal practice) contribute to institutional practices (family).

Institutional and Organizational Factors

As we mentioned earlier, in an open-class system, it is theoretically possible for individuals to significantly improve their socioeconomic position. In reality, however, this seldom happens. One reason for this is that institutions operate in such a way that the existing structures are reinforced and maintained. If we look closely, we see that social institutions operate in such a way that almost ensures that the rich stay rich and the poor stay poor.

A concrete example of institutional discrimination that supports this structure is "tax loopholes" that benefit the rich and corporations. *Google Inc.*, for example, cut its taxes by billions by moving its foreign profits to Bermuda, which levies no corporate taxes. Other corporations offer their CEOs huge salaries and bonuses. Even during the economic crisis in the late 2010s, most CEOs did not suffer. In 2010, Wall Street's top five firms gave out $90 billion in bonuses. According to one source, this was more than the Gross Domestic Product (GDP) of 13 countries.

But this is the proverbial tip of the iceberg. You may be surprised to learn that the tax rate for the richest is lower than that for lower-class and middle-class families. Obviously the rich pay more money in taxes, but they are taxed at a lower rate. Warren Buffett, one of the world's richest men, admitted that his tax rate (17.7%) was lower than that for anyone who works for him, including his secretary, whose tax rate was 30 percent. Buffett, incidentally, added that he had no particular tax planning and no "tax shelters," but his tax rate under the current system was still far lower than the tax rate for much poorer tax payers.

One reason why the wealth at the very top does not trickle down to those below is that the very top comprises a very small and very close group and breaking into this group is nearly impossible. G. William Domhoff, who examined **interlocking directorates** (the linkages among corporations that are formed by individuals who sit on multiple corporate boards), found that at the heart of this corporate and upper class culture is a small group of individuals that he called the **power elite**. These few individuals wield extraordinary power and possess astonishing wealth. By accessing a fascinating Web site (theyrule.net), you can see for yourself just how connected these individuals are to various corporations and even nonprofits.

We have given an overview of those at the top of the socioeconomic ladder and how institutional practices serve to keep them at the top, but what keeps others at the bottom? Here again we find institutional practices that converge to help sustain economic inequality. One in particular is a capitalist system that operates in a manner that ensures profits go into the hands of business owners, not employees. This practice is obvious when you study worker wages. In 2011, the United States government set the **minimum wage** at $7.25 per hour. This rate is far below what scholars refer to as the **living wage**, or the amount individuals must earn to support themselves and their families. For instance, if you and your spouse lived in Orlando, Florida, with two children, you would need to earn $28.42 per hour to afford shelter, clothing, food, and other basics. In other words, even if you worked three full-time jobs at minimum wage, you still would not earn enough to afford these basics. Put another way, you could work 24 hours per day, 7 days per week for the entire year at minimum wage and earn $63,336, which is only $4000 more than what a family of four needs to live in Orlando.

Another complicating factor is that minimum-wage or other low-wage jobs are much less likely to include medical health insurance benefits. Data from the most recent U.S. Census show that over 46 million Americans are not covered by health insurance. Among those earning less than $7.85 per hour in private industry, only 25 percent had access to medical health insurance benefits. By contrast, the rate for persons earning $34.79 or more per hour was 90 percent. Thus, those who can least afford to go to a doctor pay more to do so. The Census data also showed that 46 percent of persons working in service occupations—a

Wage Calculation for Orange County, Florida

In Orlando, Florida, a living wage for a married family with two children is $28.42 per hour, a rate far higher than the state minimum hourly wage. In the table below, you can see how these wages break down by family composition. (You can see what the living wage where you live is by visiting http://www. livingwage.geog.psu.edu/).

Hourly Wages	One Adult	One Adult, One Child	Two Adults	Two Adults, One Child	Two Adults, Two Children
Living Wage	$9.38	$17.34	$14.02	$21.98	$28.42
Minimum Wage	$7.25	$7.25	$7.25	$7.25	$7.25

Source: http://www.livingwage.geog.psu.edu/counties/12095

major growth sector of the economy—do not have access to employer-provided medical health insurance.

Consider another common employment practice that contributes to social inequality: the **Last-in First-Out** (LIFO) employment practice. When companies go through economic booms, they hire more employees; when they go through difficulties or restructuring, they usually dismiss their most recently hired employees. This practice has been particularly hard on immigrants, who are hired during economic upturns to fill a surplus of jobs and hired into the lowest-paying jobs, which tend to be least stable. During economic downturns, the surplus jobs (even those that pay very little) disappear.

The bottom line here is that it is nearly impossible to get ahead when you have barely enough to live on and are simultaneously being "nickel and dimed," as Barbara Ehrenreich calls it in her 2008 book on this subject. Where do you even start? Perhaps you decide to go to college in the hopes of getting a good job when you graduate but this is likely to result in significant student debt. In short, viewing education as a means to an end that includes making a decent living is not realistic. And because current institutional and organizational practices give some but not all a fair chance to make a decent living, economic inequality will persist.

Cultural Ideology

Class structures and economic inequality are also supported and legitimated by **cultural ideology**, the collective beliefs about the rightness of certain cultural practices. Ideology provides justification for systems or practices, no matter how illogical or immoral they may be. Our current-day open-class system is supported by the ideology of a meritocracy. **Meritocracy** is the belief that personal and professional successes are based on achievement and merit earned through hard work alone. But meritocracy gives us only the illusion of equality because it completely overlooks the myriad forms of privilege that certain groups enjoy, whether or not there is any merit to what they actually do. The concept of meritocracy also blinds us to the millions of people who, despite their hard work and determination, are unable to escape their circumstances and advance to a higher class status.

And yet, most Americans strongly believe in this ideology. Evidence of this can be found in responses to a survey conducted by the Economic Mobility Project. The goal of this survey was to determine Americans' beliefs about the American Dream. When asked if they agreed or disagreed that it's still possible for people to improve their economic standing despite the current recession, about 80 percent said it was. They also expressed the belief that hard work is the most important factor affecting economic mobility. In fact, 92 percent agreed that hard work was very important, compared to just 44 percent who believed knowing the right people is essential, or 28 percent who thought coming from a wealthy family was very important.

But it is easy to show how this belief in meritocracy is more ideology than reality. For example, one of the main reasons that people struggle to get ahead is that not everyone starts out with the same resources. Sociologist Michael Schwalbe, author of *Rigging the Game*, suggests it's analogous to putting two people into a running race and giving one of them great coaching, a nutritious diet, and good shoes, while the other is provided no coaching and has to run with weights on! Schwalbe concludes:

> Even if the rare combination of ability, effort, and luck occasionally produces a "winner" from among those starting from behind, that hardly means the game is fair—anyone who makes such a claim is offering a pep talk or a sermon or engaging in self-congratulations. What they are not doing is describing how the social world really works.

Schwalbe also points out that one reason not everyone can get ahead is that it's simply impossible for everyone to do so, even if they were to do everything right. In other words, you can't move up into the upper class unless there's room, and there's only so much room in that tiny elite group.

A related ideology is the notion that everyone should "pull themselves up by their own bootstraps." The general message is that we are all capable of doing anything, and we are ultimately in charge of our own destiny. This ideology is reflected in the negative perceptions of and lack of support for social services directed at the poorer members of society. Research by Michael McClain and his colleagues at Iowa State University shows that despite having only average or poor knowledge of the welfare system (e.g., being able to identify programs such as Medicaid correctly) most young people have negative opinions about the welfare system and about welfare recipients in particular. In fact, most young people are not even aware that the "welfare" program has been replaced by a program called TANF—Temporary Assistance for Needy Families.

But the perception that those who are poor are lazy and that they simply need to put in some good hard work and learn to take care of themselves to change their economic circumstances does not take into consideration the increased cost of living, an absence of living wages and benefits, lack of affordable housing, downturn in the economy, and so on. And all of these factors contribute to the growth of a segment of the American population that is now designated the **working poor**. This group comprises people who work but nevertheless fall below the poverty line or those who work and earn enough to be above the official poverty line but are still unable to cover their living expenses. They are living proof that it's not always about whether one is willing to work hard.

Further complicating issues related to social class is the fact that the U.S. employment market continues to pay women and racial minorities less than it pays white men for similar or identical work. Less income amounts to greater financial hardships and less chance for advancing in social class. Another way that researchers have uncovered institutional discrimination is by demonstrating that certain groups, on average, pay more for retail items than other groups. In their study "Gender and race discrimination in retail car negotiations," Ian Ayres and Peter Siegelman found that automobile dealers made much better initial and final offers to white men than they did to black men, black women, or white women. Similar trends have been documented in relation to purchasing homes, renting apartments, and even daily expenditures such as personal care items and dry cleaning. In other words, those who earn less, pay more.

Examples like this also reveal that social class inequality is supported by cultural ideology. When cultural ideology supports the idea that everyone should get ahead and further supports the "pull yourself up by the bootstraps" philosophy, there appears to be no reason to change the system.

Interpersonal Factors

Interpersonal communication and interactions can also reinforce existing values and practices. For instance, when car dealers discriminate against women or minorities in negotiating a deal, they help perpetuate social class inequality by making it harder for those who already tend to be disadvantaged to get ahead, even if they are not aware that they are doing it. But one of the most important and influential forms of interpersonal communication and interaction that may contribute to social class inequality is that which occurs between parent and child—i.e., parental socialization of children.

Sociologist Annette Lareau studied ways that parents from different social class backgrounds raised their children. She found that middle-class children are taught self-direction, curiosity and independence, while working-class children learn conformity and following the rules. Working-class children learn to be neat, clean, and obey the rules at home and school. Middle-class children are more comfortable with authority figures and are more likely to negotiate actively with parents, teachers, and other authority figures. They learn that their future success depends on such assertiveness and initiative. Because they are socialized to engage in conversation with adults, to reason their way through conflicts, and to question authority figures, they tend to be more comfortable in public and display more confidence than working-class children.

These basic differences in socialization have far-reaching implications for children's futures. Middle-class children will have distinct advantages when they move into the workplace, at least in those jobs that reward assertiveness, ingenuity, the ability to deal well with people in power, and so on. If you think about it, those are sought after characteristics in jobs that tend to pay more. The jobs that reward following the rules, being obedient to authority, and so on, are likely to be relatively low paying, for example, factory work or waiting tables.

Lareau found that middle-class parents sought to "cultivate" their children's talents and interests in a "concerted" fashion and labeled the process by which middle-class children are socialized **concerted cultivation**. Such parents, she discovered, would ask questions of their children and be interested in their opinions. It was okay if the child disagreed with them. Middle-class children were also involved with many extracurricular activities, and children could transfer the skills and attitudes they learned in these activities into advanced education or employment arenas.

In contrast, Lareau found that children of working-class or poor parents were socialized via the **accomplishment of natural growth** model. Rather than guiding children's actions, parents were more likely to let children develop "naturally." As a rule, the children spent more time without parental supervision. Lareau argues that although there's nothing innately inferior about this parenting style, it does not prepare children as well for the workplace and higher education, where verbal skills, initiative, assertiveness, and so on, are all highly valued. In using the natural growth approach, parents are simply preparing their children for the types of jobs that they themselves hold (i.e., parents teach children what they know and do, thereby reproducing their social class).

Individual-Level Factors

Thus far, our discussion of social class inequality has revealed how inequality is based in organizational, cultural, and interpersonal processes and practices. This is important to remember because it suggests that remedies to reduce gross economic inequalities will require system-wide changes, not just changes in a few people's attitudes and behavior. But it is individuals that make up all those organizations, cultures, and interpersonal relationships, so it is important to consider how individuals help to maintain systems of inequality.

One obvious way that individuals contribute to social inequality is by harboring negative opinions about the poor or TANF recipients and by failing to see how their own lives benefit from social programs. Moreover, people who are angry about their tax dollars being used to help welfare recipients often have no problem enjoying the social benefits of state taxes that pay for highways, police and fire protection, public libraries, public education, Social Security and Medicare, federal emergency assistance, a military, and many more aspects of social life that are made available through public taxes and government assistance. Many of these same people also fail to understand that the line between middle-class economic comfort and lower-class economic woe is a very thin line indeed. Consider, for example, the fascinating discovery of sociologist Mark Rank, who studies poverty trends in the United States. Poverty and welfare, Rank claims, are as American as apple pie. . . . Most of us will experience poverty during our lives. Even more surprising, most Americans will turn to public assistance at least once during adulthood. Rather than poverty and welfare use being an issue of them, it is more an issue of us.

Despite Rank's assertions, many Americans continue to be uninformed about poverty and welfare and assume that welfare recipients are unwilling to work and prefer to "live off the taxpayer." But reality paints a different picture. For instance, approximately 1 in 5 children currently live in poverty (these individuals are not *able* to work legally). Moreover, the major difficulty low-income parents (and especially single parents) face is not in keeping or finding a job but in finding affordable child care. And there are countless people work two jobs but still do not make enough to support their families.

Of course, there are always people who will take advantage of any system (although welfare laws severely limit how long individuals can receive government assistance), but this can and does happen at all levels, not just among the poor. For example, very few people are aware of the myriad ways in which the wealthy (including corporations) benefit from government assistance. Perhaps the best examples of government assistance are the tax rates and tax breaks offered to wealthy people and corporations. The end result of these tax practices mirrors the purpose of TANF: governmental policies provide financial assistance to certain people/groups (regardless of whether or not the assistance is "needs-based"). The more we stay informed and know the facts about poverty (and about where government assistance goes and what it does), the less likely we are to perpetuate economic inequality through prejudice and ignorance.

CONSEQUENCES OF CLASS STRATIFICATION

Virtually every aspect of people's lives—their health, educational opportunities, working conditions, childbearing, marital happiness—is influenced by their social class position. In this section, we discuss two broad arenas shaped by income and class position—health and education.

Health Outcomes

Because the United States does not have a comprehensive system of universal health care, many Americans do not have health coverage. Indeed, according to the U.S. Census Bureau, the number of people without health insurance coverage in 2008 was 46.3 million (15.4 percent of the U.S. population). In 2009, the number of people without health insurance coverage had grown to 50.7 million (16.7 percent). This included 7.5 million children under the age of 18 (10 percent). But if we look at only the poorest children in this country, the rate is 15.1 percent. This is rather clear evidence that income affects access to health care insurance and (by extension) to health care. Corroborating evidence comes from the U.S. Census Bureau, which reports that the percentage of uninsured individuals decreases as household income increases. The percent of uninsured persons in households with incomes less than $25,000 per year was 26.6 compared to 9.1 percent in households earning $75,000 or more.

Inadequate health care coverage creates a ripple effect. According to a study published in the *New England Journal of Medicine*, researcher David Baker and his colleagues found that lack of insurance leads to greater declines in overall health among middle-aged adults. In addition, the National Academies of Sciences released a report that found that communities with high rates of uninsured persons suffer from reduced access to hospital services, reduced funding for disease prevention, and other outcomes that affect all community residents, not just the uninsured. The report notes:

> It is misguided and even dangerous to assume that lack of health insurance harms only those who are uninsured. . . . The rest of the community pays for uncompensated medical care either directly or indirectly, and high rates of uninsurance can strain community health systems to the point that important services have to be cut or eliminated.

Lack of insurance translates into lack of preventive care (e.g., annual check-ups that may lead to early detection of disease) and lack of medical treatment for acute and chronic illnesses. Unquestionably, this lack of health insurance contributes to the many negative health outcomes associated with lower-income status. These outcomes include lower life expectancy, higher infant mortality, and generally poorer health.

Life expectancy—the average number of years an individual is likely to live—is linked to income. In the U.S., the average life expectancy is about 78 years. Research has found, however, that those with higher incomes live longer. Thus, **premature mortality** is more likely for those with lower incomes. In addition, **morbidity** (e.g., poor health, disabilities) is also linked to income. For example, obesity rates are much higher among lower-income persons than those who earn more.

At the other end of the life cycle—infancy—we also see the effects of income. You may be shocked to learn that the United States has one of the highest **infant mortality rates** (IMR) of all wealthy nations. IMR is the number of children dying under age 1 divided by the number of live births in a given year. In one study comparing infant mortality rates in 4 major cities (New York City, London, Paris, and Tokyo), only in the United States was the link between infant mortality and income clearly evident. The researchers argue that lack of adequate health care to mothers in poor neighborhoods in the United States (the only country studied that lacked comprehensive/universal health care) mainly accounts for this effect.

Infant Mortality Rates by Selected Countries

Country	Deaths per 1000 live births
United States	6.14
Cuba	5.72
Canada	4.99
Australia	4.67
France	3.31
Japan	2.79
Singapore	2.32

Source: Central Intelligence Agency (CIA). *The World Factbook.* https://www.cia.gov/library/publications/the-world-factbook/rankorder/2091rank.html

Educational Outcomes

Health is not the only area where income matters. Educational opportunities and quality of education are also determined by social class. Wealthier families have the ability to send their children to private schools that almost always provide superior educational opportunities when compared to public schools, the latter being largely underfunded. According to the National Association of Independent Schools, in 2008–2009 the median tuition for private schools (not including boarding schools) was $17,441 (tuition at boarding schools was about $37,000). Even with scholarships, which are limited and often given only to the top students, private schools are out of reach for most people. And while there are undoubtedly some great public schools, these schools are not likely to be found in the poorest neighborhoods.

Educational opportunities start before a child enters school, of course. Families that can afford quality preschool for their children help ensure that their children are "school ready" when they do start school. Not surprisingly, one study found that families enrolling their children in quality preschool programs earned $2,000 more per month than families whose children were not in preschool. When children enter kindergarten not knowing their letters and numbers, they are already behind their preschooled peers and more likely to fail down the road. This same pattern can be seen in high school dropout rates. Among 16–24 year olds from families with income in the lowest 25 percent of all Americans, there is a 16.4 percent dropout rate (nearly twice the national average). Conversely, among individuals in the highest income quartile, the dropout rate is only 2.2 percent.

As the statistics above indicate, the link between income level and educational attainment occurs at all levels—from preschool to higher education.

Because educational levels affect occupation and income (the better and higher the educational level, the higher the occupational status and income), a vicious cycle emerges. Lower income results in lower educational attainment, which in turn results in lower income. Scholarships and student loans can help close the gap between the "haves" and the "have nots" by enabling children from lower- and working-class families to attend college. However, today's average college graduate leaves college not just with a diploma but also with a huge debt. In 2009, according to the Project on Student Debt, the average college graduate carried $24,000 of student debt into the workplace. This sum is undoubtedly higher among lower- and working-class families because they more frequently lack the means to pay for their children's education outright and must borrow more than their middle-class counterparts. Starting out adult life in substantial debt keeps the cycle of poverty turning.

SUMMARY

Economic stratification (a significant form of social stratification) can take on various forms depending upon historical and cultural circumstances. In the United States, it assumes the form of an open-class system that (at least in theory) allows everyone to move up or down the socioeconomic ladder. As we've seen, however, the reality is that most people do not change their social positions in radical ways. One reason for this is that economic stratification is built into the fabric of society. As such, it is maintained and reinforced at all levels—organizational, institutional, ideological, and interpersonal. Thus, social class remains one of the most fundamental ways in which individuals are differentiated in the United States and it shapes lives in profound ways. Those at the upper rungs of the socioeconomic ladder enjoy longer and healthier lives; those at the bottom are likely to suffer from a variety of mental and physical illnesses and die younger. Most sociologists and economists see few signs that the disparities in health and other lifestyle behaviors between the rich and poor will decline, especially because the income gap between rich and poor is widening.

Further Reading

Chaudry, Ajay. *Putting Children First: How Low-wage Working Mothers Manage Child Care.* New York: Russell Sage Foundation, 2004.

Domhoff, G. William. *Power in America: Interlocking Directorates in the Corporate Community, 2005.* http://sociology.ucsc.edu/whorulesamerica/power/corporate_community.html

Domhoff, G. William. *Who Rules America? Power and Politics and Social Change.* Boston, Mass.: McGraw-Hill, 2006.

Ehrenreich, Barbara. *Nickel and Dimed: On (Not) Getting By in America.* New York: Henry Holt & Co., 2008.

Gilbert, Dennis L. *The American Class Structure in an Age of Growing Inequality*. Los Angeles: Pine Forge Press, 2011.

Goldin, Claudia Dale, and Lawrence F. Katz. 2008. *The Race Between Education and Technology*. Cambridge, Mass: Belknap Press of Harvard University Press.

Levitt, Steven D., and Stephen J. Dubner. *Freakonomics: A Rogue Economist Explores the Hidden Side of Everything*. New York: William Morrow, 2005.

Massey, Douglas S. *Categorically Unequal: The American Stratification System*. New York: Russell Sage Foundation, 2008.

Rank, Mark R. "As American as Apple Pie: Poverty and Welfare." *Contexts* 2 (2003):41–49.

CHAPTER 3

RACIAL AND ETHNIC STRATIFICATION

As you are undoubtedly aware, a historical election took place in November 2008. For the first time in U.S. history, a bi-racial President was elected. Almost immediately, some media and Internet sources rushed to declare an "end to racism." What could be better proof that African Americans had finally gained equality in America than the ascendancy of a black man to the highest political office. (Ironically, the President is never referred to as bi-racial or white, even though he is as much white as black)

Just a few months later, in July of 2009, Harvard University professor Henry Louis Gates, Jr. was arrested at his home in Cambridge, Massachusetts, after a neighbor saw someone trying to enter Gates' home and called the police, thinking a burglary might be in progress. The man trying to open the jammed door was Gates, the homeowner. Gates is black. Whether or not the neighbor would have called police if the man trying to open the door was white is unclear, but this incident did bring to a head the issue of **racial profiling**—the practice of police singling out of members of racial or ethnic minority groups for questioning or interrogation, based upon nothing or little more than their race/ethnicity. Almost immediately, everyone began talking about how racism is alive and well in the United States.

Two "racial" incidents, just a few months apart, suggest very different realities. The media are always chasing a story, of course, and both of these incidents lend themselves to sensationalism. But what these examples also make clear is that race and race relations in the United States are very complex issues.

There is no question that race relations in the United States have improved considerably—how else can we account for President Obama's victory? But racial stratification and inequality are also very real in contemporary society and help account for such things as racial profiling and other discriminatory practices, prejudice, racial violence, and lack of opportunities and resources in many people's lives. How both of these realities can co-exist in one place, in one historic period, leads us to one of the most interesting topics of social stratification—racial inequality.

SOCIOLOGICAL PERSPECTIVES ON RACE AND ETHNICITY

Everyone knows what race is . . . *or do they*? For the most part, individuals determine race on the basis of **phenotypes**, or observable characteristics such as hair color, skin color, shape of eyes, and so on. We assume that members of particular racial groups share certain physical characteristics that distinguish them from members of other groups. For example, blacks are thought to have darker skin and hair than other groups, the eyes of Asians tend to be more almond-shaped than rounded, and so on. These physical differences are the result of adaptations to physical environments. For instance, the most obvious racial feature—skin color—is a function of the amount of melanin in the skin. **Melanin** is the pigment found in our skin and is the source of our skin color. Those with a greater concentration of melanin have darker skin, and those with limited melanin have lighter skin. Over time, groups who lived or settled near the equator, where the sun's ultraviolet rays are most intense, maintained high levels of melanin to protect them from these harmful rays.

It seems obvious then that race is biological, or at least a biological adaptation to environmental conditions. But things are not always as clear as they seem. One of the most perplexing and important facts about race is that there is as much variation *within* a particular racial group as there is *between* two "distinct" racial groups. For example, among individuals who identify as black, there are some that are lighter skinned and have lighter colored hair than persons who identify as "white." Some physical features that seem distinct to one group can be found in another, distant racial group. For instance, Scandinavians share the same nose shape as Nilote Africans. In short, there is no physical or biological feature that appears only in one racial group. Indeed, there is no "race gene," although there are certain **alleles**, or gene variants, that tend to be associated more with one group than another.

Take another example. Certain diseases, such as sickle-cell anemia and cystic fibrosis, are thought to be race-specific. But while it is true that sickle-cell anemia is more likely to occur among African Americans, the disease does occur in other populations (e.g., Mediterranean) and is practically nonexistent in some African countries. Cystic fibrosis, a so-called "white disease," is actually found in all populations. Some of this cross-over of so-called "race-specific" diseases may result from mixed heritage, but the fact remains that even though there is a greater likelihood of certain traits or conditions being associated with a particular racial group, there is far more similarity among persons of different races than difference, and certainly more than commonly assumed.

To make matters even more confusing, definitions or classifications of race change frequently. The U.S. Census Bureau has collected data on race since 1790, but virtually every census has measured race differently. In 2010, for instance, there were 14 races identified (who knew there were so many?). In 2000, however, there were actually 63 possible racial identities from which individuals could choose, because individuals could, for the first time, pick multiple races, not just one, even though there were just five primary races and one "other" from which to choose (the 2010 census also allowed individuals to choose multiple races). It should also be noted that race is categorized differently in other countries, sometimes with greater or fewer classifications. When the Spanish colonized Mexico, for instance, they created a system with 16 racial categories, none of which is identical to those used in the United States today.

Definitions of race change over time; indeed, it is possible for an individual's race to change over the course of his or her lifetime. Gregory Williams was actually white when he was growing up in Virginia in the 1940s but "became" black when he moved to Indiana at the age of 10. In his moving memoir, *Life on the Color Line: The True Story of a White Boy Who Discovered He Was Black*, Gregory recalls the shock and confusion of learning that he was not who he had thought he was. Gregory grew up with the understanding that to have dark skin was to be black. At the age of 10, he suddenly discovered that his light-skinned father was black. Gregory soon learned that he would face a dual challenge: growing up to be perceived by many as a white man, but also being encouraged by family members not to "forget where you came from when you livin' high on the hog." As Gregory learned at a young age, race is a fluid concept and continues to evolve with social and political changes.

Many individuals think of race and ethnicity as the same thing, but these concepts have different meanings to the government and social scientists. **Race** is a social construct that refers to a group of people who share some sort of outwardly defining physical characteristics or ancestry. **Ethnicity** generally refers to aspects of culture (e.g., food, clothing, language) that distinguish one group from another. It is easy to see how race and ethnicity could be confused as styles of clothing, music, food, and language are often associated with particular races. Generally speaking, however, racial classifications rely on *continental* groups, and ethnicities distinguish groups within those continents.

Interestingly, in the United States, only two ethnicities are formally recognized—Hispanic and non-Hispanic—even though there are many groups that share a cultural heritage and could be said to share ethnicity (e.g., Jews, the Irish, Italians). In the United States, because race and ethnicity are considered distinct, people can share ethnicity but be of different races. Consider the U.S. Puerto Rican population, for example. Historically, Puerto Ricans comprised three different racial groups who lived or settled on the island of Puerto Rico: white Europeans from Spain, black Africans who were brought to the Caribbean during the slave trade, and a group of natives known as Taino. Depending upon attributes or ancestry, Puerto Ricans can identify as white/Hispanic, black/Hispanic, American Indian/Hispanic, or even a combination of these (i.e., multiracial/Hispanic).

It is important to recognize that, just as with racial classifications, there is no biological basis for ethnicity and the recognition of just two ethnicities is somewhat arbitrary, although it can be traced historically to migratory patterns. But we could just as easily recognize multiple ethnicities, or none at all. Hispanic or Latino could be classified as a race, not an ethnicity. Again, ethnicity, like race, can be defined in multiple ways, and any system used to define groups by ethnicity inevitably ignores the complexity and richness of people's lives.

If race (or ethnicity) had a clear biological basis, an individual's race (or ethnicity) would not change just because family circumstances change or because a person was born a generation earlier or later. For these reasons, sociologists argue that race and ethnicity are social constructions, not biological facts. In other words, race and ethnicity are concepts that develop within a culture and as such, ideas about race and ethnicity vary across cultures and historical periods. Both race and ethnicity are far more significant as social concepts than biological ones. Furthermore, the common insistence among many that race is biological can be seen as a rationale for the differential treatment of people on the basis of race. If you believe that Asians are genetically smarter or that blacks are genetically superior athletes but less intelligent than other groups, then it becomes easier to treat individuals differently on the basis of race. If you accept that race and ethnicity are social constructions, as sociologists do, then the differential treatment of people on the basis of their race or ethnicity, as well as different life circumstances among various groups, becomes problematic, especially since such differences have very real and serious consequences for people's lives.

STRATIFICATION BY RACE AND ETHNICITY

Social stratification refers to the uneven distribution of resources and power within society. Individuals or groups are stratified, or ranked, according to their access to or control over desired resources. Those at the top of the stratification ladder enjoy greater material comforts and pleasures and are held in higher esteem than those lower in rank. To say that society is stratified by race suggests that wealth, prestige, and power vary noticeably between racial groups. One does not need to look very far to see that racial stratification is a key organizing feature of contemporary society.

Obviously there are some very powerful and wealthy persons in society who are also members of minority groups. Oprah Winfrey, for example, was at one time the only black billionaire in the world (according to *Forbes International Billionaire List*). Latino Carlos Slim, CEO of several major corporations and the largest shareholder of the New York Times Company, was listed on the *2009 Time 100 List* of the most influential people in the world; in 2010, he became the richest man in the world (worth $53.5 billion) when he bumped Bill Gates into second place. But the success of a few individuals is not evidence of racial equality in terms of wealth and poverty. In fact, the very uneven distribution of wealth in society is strongly associated with race and ethnicity.

In terms of income levels, Asian Americans tend to have the highest income, followed by non-Hispanic whites, Hispanics, and finally blacks. The difference between the highest median income households and the lowest is about $31,400. Although this figure may seem meaningless, especially if you have not established your own household, here is what $31,400 could buy you:

- Tuition and fees for a four-year undergraduate degree in most public universities in the United States
- A 14-day cruise for four to Antarctica
- A new 2011 Volkswagen Passat with enough money left over to pay for a year's worth of gas and oil changes
- Down payment and closing costs on a brand new 2,500 square foot home in many urban centers (valued at $260,000)
- 31 weekend vacations for two at the elegant Bellagio Hotel in Las Vegas, Nevada (every other weekend for a year)
- The 2010 world's largest TV—a revolutionary 152-inch Panasonic full-HD 3-D TV with enough money left over to buy a premium 7.1 channel home theater system, matching Blu-ray player, and 275 of your favorite Blu-ray movies

Median Family Income by Race in 2008

Asian: 65,637

White, non-Hispanic: 55,530

Hispanic (any race): 37,913

Black: 34,218

Source: U.S. Census Bureau, *Current Population Reports,* 2009.

On the other end of the economic spectrum, data from the U.S. Census Bureau show that in 2010, approximately 15.1 percent of all persons living in the United States were considered to be below poverty level but also showed considerable variation by race. About 13 percent of all whites lived below the poverty line, but for non-Hispanic whites, the rate was 9.9 percent. For blacks, nearly 27 percent lived below poverty; for Asians, this rate was about 12.1 percent. Among Hispanics (any race), the rate was 26.6 percent. If we break this down further and look at families headed by single women, the differences in rates are even more pronounced: Hispanic and African American households headed by women are far more likely to live in poverty compared to non-Hispanic white and Asian-American households headed by women.

One important indicator of social stratification is political power. Almost all of the incoming members of the U.S. House of Representatives elected in 2010 are white. This incoming class is no different from Congress as a whole in terms of race, that is, whites far outnumber minority group members in the U.S. Congress. At the time of this writing, there were only four racial minority senators in the U.S. Senate: two Hispanic and two Asian. In the House of Representatives, there are 42 African Americans, 2 Hispanics, and 9 Asians. For a basis of comparison, we should reiterate that there are a grand total of 100 senators and 435 representatives at the federal level in the U.S. Although the United

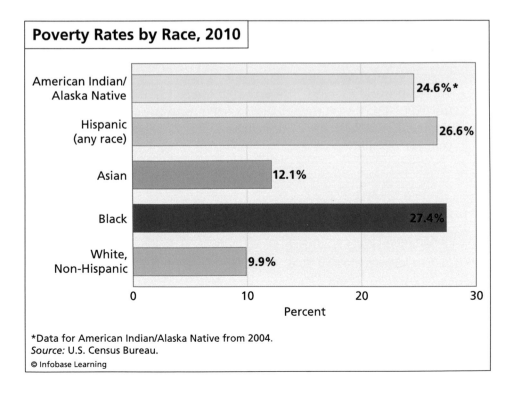

Poverty Rates by Race, 2010

American Indian/Alaska Native: 24.6%*
Hispanic (any race): 26.6%
Asian: 12.1%
Black: 27.4%
White, Non-Hispanic: 9.9%

Percent

*Data for American Indian/Alaska Native from 2004.
Source: U.S. Census Bureau.
© Infobase Learning

States elected a bi-racial president in 2008 (President Obama's father was black, his mother was white), Obama is recognized as the first and only bi-racial president in our nation's 230-plus year history.

In sum, despite the fact that there are a few powerful and wealthy minorities and some very poor whites, wealth and prestige are strongly associated with race and ethnicity. In terms of income, non-Hispanic whites and Asian Americans tend to enjoy greater financial security than other minority groups, and non-Hispanic whites hold most positions of power within corporations and government.

HOW RACIAL STRATIFICATION IS MAINTAINED

Sociologists reject biological explanations for racial stratification. In other words, they do not believe that stratification stems from any type of biological differences between racial groups or that biology is a factor in determining intelligence or motivation. As previously noted, biological differences between races are quite minimal and those differences that do exist do not in and of themselves account for the wide variations in wealth and power that we see in contemporary society. Instead, racial stratification is maintained through certain key social and institutional forces and dynamics. These include prejudice and discrimination, violence, and institutional racism.

Prejudice and Discrimination

Sociologists use the term **racial prejudice** to refer specifically to negative judgments about a particular racial group. These judgments are often formed before an individual even has close interactions with members of a given group and can be extremely resistant to change. Prejudice describes *thoughts and feelings* about members of another group, but not actions toward them. **Discrimination**, on the other hand, is *behavior* that results in unfair treatment of a person or group on the basis of their group membership. Both discrimination and prejudice are usually grounded in **racial stereotypes**, or exaggerated and oversimplified beliefs about members of a particular racial group (e.g., most Native Americans are alcoholic, all Asian Americans are smart).

Because prejudice is so ingrained, many people do not recognize their own attitudes as racist or will insist that their attitudes are grounded in cause. They can cite examples from the past that reinforce their perceptions—for example, the Latino friend from high school who joined a gang or the Chinese-American student who was class valedictorian. What they fail to recognize or remember is that the vast majority of Latinos in their high school were not gang members and that there were plenty of Asian American students who did not graduate at the top of their class.

The problem then is that because many people do not recognize themselves as having racist attitudes, these attitudes go unchecked and can shape behaviors in significant ways. Consider research conducted by Bertrand and Mullaina-than ("Are Greg and Emily More Employable than Lakisha and Jamal?"). These researchers submitted four sets of resumes to help-wanted ads in Boston and Chicago. The four sets of resumes contained equivalent education and job histories. The only difference between the resumes in each of the four sets was the use of a name more typical to a specific race and/or gender. Names like Greg and Emily were used for the "white" resumes, while names like Lakisha and Jamal were used for the "black" resumes. Out of the nearly 5,000 resumes sent out, 10 percent of those with "white" names received a call-back, while only 6.7 percent of those with "black" names received a call-back. The only jobs for which resumes with "black" names received more call-backs than for "white" were for transportation and communication jobs. The call-back rates for all other types of jobs (finance, managerial, health, etc.) were substantially higher for "white" resumes.

The study by Ayres and Siegelman (see Chapter 2), which explored whether car dealers discriminated against women and racial minorities interested in buying a new car shows similar prejudicial and discriminatory responses. The researchers found that dealers made much better initial and final offers to white males than they did to black males, black women or white women. For instance, compared to prices offered white men, the prices quoted were about $200 higher for white women, $400 higher for black women, and $900 higher for black men. Even after negotiating, the final markup price was 50 percent higher for white women, twice as much for black women and four times as much for black men, as compared to white men. Ayres and Siegelman noted that "without any negotiating at all, two out of five white males obtained a better offer than their counterparts achieved after bargaining on average for more than forty minutes."

It should be obvious how prejudice, stereotypes, and discrimination, even at an individual level, serve to maintain racial stratification in society, especially if blacks or Hispanics, for example, have more difficulty finding jobs or spend more money for basic services and goods. Or imagine being Native American and interviewing for a job if the person sitting across from you believes you might be a heavy drinker. No matter how qualified you are for the job, such a stereotype would severely limit your chance at a fair interview. Even seemingly positive stereotypes, such as Asian Americans are a "model minority," can be damaging because it sets high and somewhat unreal expectations for all Asian Americans to achieve success. As a result, a Japanese American may be ridiculed for earning a B or C in a high school math class, while members of another racial group may receive no such reaction for a similar grade. Additionally, this model minority stereotype is used (incorrectly) to demonstrate that success is achievable for all minority groups if only they try hard enough. In other words, the mythical treatment of Asian Americans hurts not only Asian Americans, but other racial minorities.

Keep in mind that prejudices and stereotypes are not just held by those in power; individuals of minority groups may also hold such beliefs about members of their own groups. And if these attitudes become *internalized* and shape an individual's feelings about herself or himself, it would be especially difficult to challenge or resist racial injustice and one's place in the stratification system.

Ideological Racism and Institutional Discrimination

Racial prejudice and discrimination exist on a much broader level than individual personal feelings, attitudes, and behaviors. When beliefs about the perceived inferiority of certain racial groups become woven into the fabric of a society and shared by large numbers of people, they enter into the realm of **ideological racism**. Ideological racism is the society-level equivalent of individual prejudice (see sidebar). An example of ideological racism can be seen in the explanations and justifications people once made for the existence of slavery. Slavery in the United States and other countries was accepted for centuries because whites believed blacks were innately different and inferior; there was even debate about whether blacks were "human." These widespread beliefs, or ideology, justified treating blacks inhumanely.

Discrimination has a society-level equivalent as well. **Institutional discrimination** is the term used to describe unequal treatment found within social institutions. Institutional discrimination takes place in the education system, the housing market, the employment arena, the penal system, the health care system, and all levels of government, among countless other social institutions. The laws, customs, practices, and policies that govern these institutions serve to reinforce and maintain stratification. Institutional discrimination is detrimental to entire groups because it infects the social institutions which provide the structure within which we live.

Before the Civil Rights Movement during the 1960s, institutional discrimination was easy to recognize in the United States because it pervaded the legal system. Until the 1960s, Jim Crow laws required that blacks use separate facilities from those used by whites (water fountains, public restrooms and parks),

Individual vs. Societal Prejudice and Discrimination

	Individual	Societal
Thinking/Feeling	Prejudice	Ideological racism
Doing/Acting	Discrimination	Institutional discrimination

Source: Merton, Robert. *Social Theory and Social Structure,* 1968.

attend separate schools, use different forms of transportation, and so on. Some states enacted **antimiscegenation laws** that prohibited interracial marriage, and subjected individuals to the **one drop rule**, which stated that if you had even "one drop" of black blood, then you were considered black. The **hypodescent rule** also determined that if you were of mixed-race, you were considered to belong to the "inferior" race.

Because minorities (especially blacks) lacked political power, they were subject to abuses of all sorts. One of the most egregious examples of institutional racism is the **Tuskegee syphilis experiment**. Between 1932 and 1972 the U.S. Public Health Service conducted a study of untreated syphilis. The subjects used in the studies were 399 poor African American men in Tuskegee, Alabama. Researchers failed to treat syphilitic patients who participated in the study even after it became known that penicillin was effective in treating the disease and patients. Furthermore, doctors withheld information about the disease from patients. Many of the men died from the disease and related complications, and some of their wives were infected (as well as children who contracted the disease through pregnancy or at birth).

The Civil Rights Movement led to the passage of key laws that made racial discrimination illegal (e.g., Fair Housing Act; Brown vs. Board of Education). Today, instances of overt discrimination have become less common, but they still exist. In 2009, for instance, a judge in Louisiana denied a marriage license to an interracial couple. Claiming that he wasn't racist, the judge commented that he just didn't "believe in mixing the races that way." Most institutional discrimination today operates in ways that are more subtle and therefore more difficult to track. But a little digging reveals patterns of institutional discrimination in various social settings. For instance, a reporter for the *Atlanta Journal-Constitution* examined home loan records and found that blacks were rejected more than twice as often as whites when applying for loans. Additional research on lending, housing, and jobs shows that racial discriminatory practices continue in all of these areas.

Sociologist Douglas Massey, in his book *Categorically Unequal*, argues that racial discrimination is far from over:

> ...now that naked racism is publicly condemned and discrimination is illegal, discriminatory practices have gone underground, becoming more subtle but remaining quite effective in perpetuating racial stratification. Likewise, although principled racism has waned and racist views are rarely voiced, substantial shares of whites continue to hold negative stereotypes about African Americans and unconsciously harbor negative racial sentiments that cause them to avoid contact with African Americans in families, schools, neighborhoods, churches, and other settings, yielding low levels of inter-marriage and high levels of segregation between blacks and whites.

Although Massey is referring to relations between whites and blacks, the same can be said for other groups, including Hispanics.

In his book *Racism without Racists*, Eduardo Bonilla-Silva asserts that ideological racism has simply gone underground, mostly because it is no longer acceptable to publicly display racist beliefs or opinions and people are encouraged not to recognize color. He calls this phenomenon **color-blind racism**. Bonilla-Silva further suggests that people harbor their prejudices privately without openly admitting it to others. While interviewing college students and working adults about race relations in the United States, he found that these individuals tried hard to mask racial prejudice. But Bonilla-Silva listened to *how* people talked about race, not just what they said, and he found that their language told a different story. For example, a technique that whites used to appear less prejudiced was the rhetorical phrase: "I am not prejudiced, but . . . " This was invariably followed by a biased statement. Another common technique he observed was how people stated up front: "Some of my best friends are [black, Asian]." The implication, of course, is that if you have friends of other racial groups, you clearly are not racist. But when Bonilla-Silva followed up, he learned that these black friends or Asian friends were mere acquaintances or co-workers, and individuals did not have close relationships.

Over time, people have simply learned that it is socially unacceptable to express overt racial prejudice and have simultaneously learned ways to hide overt racism behind socially acceptable verbiage. Scholars have come to refer to this new face of racism as **polite racism**—that is, we may harbor racist beliefs, but we understand that we should not blatantly express such attitudes to others. Indeed, scholars have also noticed that younger people are becoming increasingly more adept at employing carefully placed phrases and hesitant language to make themselves appear unprejudiced.

Limiting Educational Options

One of the main ways in which Americans can improve their life circumstances is by achieving higher levels of education, which opens the door to better jobs and incomes. Indeed, access to educational opportunities has helped various groups achieve greater equality. But institutional discrimination continues to exist within the educational system and this in turn helps maintain racial stratification.

Racial segregation in schools was banned in 1954 with the landmark case of *Brown v Board of Education*, but racial segregation in schools still exists. What many people fail to recognize is that although school segregation was legally banned, almost nothing was done to foster integration in public schools, and so these public schools remained segregated. In most cases, your physical address (home, apartment, shelter) determines which school you attend. And this deceptively simple fact explains why school segregation persists.

Brown v Board of Education desegregated schools, but it did nothing to desegregate housing communities. As a result, we shifted from **de jure (by law) segregation** to **de facto (in practice) segregation**. Black neighborhoods yield black student populations, and vice versa, which serves as an excellent reminder of how intertwined social institutions (in this case, housing and education) can be. Urban public schools, which are heavily populated by minority students, lack the financial and human resources necessary to educate tomorrow's leaders. As a result, from day one the students in these urban schools are at a disadvantage when compared to students who reside in more affluent, suburban neighborhoods. Jonathan Kozol, author of *Savage Inequalities*, notes numerous ways in which such inequality shapes children's opportunities. He contrasts, for instance, schools in Princeton, New Jersey (an affluent area), where (mostly white) students "have access to the use of seven well-appointed 'music suites'" with schools in Jersey City, New Jersey (a poor area), where many (mostly minority) students have no access to musical instruments and take music classes in the lunchroom or basement. In other poor districts, such as Paterson, New Jersey, there is so much overcrowding that abandoned factories are now home to four elementary schools.

These imbalanced educational experiences play out in important ways. For instance, college-bound black seniors score considerably lower on the SAT than white students. In 2009, the difference was 209 points. As you know, in a competitive academic world where just +/- 30 points can make or break a student's chance of college acceptance, a 209 point differential is enormous. Not surprisingly, we find that Hispanic non-whites and black Americans are less likely to attain degrees at all levels (see sidebar).

It is important to note an exception to this pattern. Asian American students, as a group, tend to perform better than all racial groups, including white students. For example, their average SAT scores are 39 points higher than those of white students. However, according to a College Board report entitled *Asian*

Highest Level of Education Attained by Race/Ethnicity: 2008

	High School Completion	Bachelors	Masters	Doctorate
White	90.6%	30.2%	10.3%	1.2%
Black	82.1%	17.5%	5.2%	0.5%
Hispanic	63.1%	11.7%	3.3%	0.25%

Source: National Center for Education Statistics (2008)

Americans and Pacific Islander: Facts, Not Fiction, academic success for this "model" group is closely tied to both socioeconomic status and parental education. On average, Asian American students whose parents have no high school diploma or whose parents make less than $20,000 per year scored about 440 on the verbal portion of the SAT, compared to about 570 for Asian American students whose parents hold a graduate degree and/or make more than $100,000 per year.

There are many reasons why blacks, Hispanics, and Native Americans achieve less in school than their white and Asian counterparts, not all of them connected to ideological racism or institutional discrimination within the schools. The fact that urban youth belong overwhelmingly to poor and working-class families who have neither the time nor the money to develop children's capabilities outside of the public school system certainly contributes to the problem. Regardless of the reasons, the fact that educational outcomes for racial minorities (with the exception of Asian Americans) are more limited helps to perpetuate racial stratification.

Racial Violence and Hate Crimes

One of the most disturbing yet effective ways to maintain racial stratification is violence, or the threat of violence. Sadly, the United States has a long history of racial violence, starting even before the country was formally established. Native Americans were among the first victims of racial violence in what would become the United States. Many Native Americans were killed in the country's early days—by direct violence, by diseases introduced by the colonists, and by forced migration. It is estimated that Native Americans had a population of at least 1 million in 1492, but that population fell to less than 250,000 by 1900. Some of the worst violence was perpetrated by the U.S. government, which sought to acquire land occupied by Native Americans. The most famous and deadly case was an event known as the **Trail of Tears**, which involved the relocation of thousands of Native Americans from their lands to "Indian Territory." In route, thousands died from disease, starvation, and exposure to cold. Almost all Native Americans who resisted being relocated (such as those known now as Seminole Indians in Florida) were forcibly removed from their lands or killed. Later, violence was directed at non-white immigrants, who were competing with whites for jobs during the 18th and 19th centuries. In 1862, for instance, 88 Chinese Americans were murdered; it is likely that this number accounts for reported incidents only and that there were many more deaths that went unreported.

Violence, and the threat of violence, was used to establish (in the case of Native Americans) and maintain (in the case of non-white immigrants) **white supremacy**, a system based on the underlying premise that whites are superior to other racial groups and thereby retain power and control by virtue of this perceived superiority. After slavery was abolished, violence continued to be used as a means to keep African Americans in subordinate positions. Robert Gibson, author of the 1979 book *The Negro Holocaust*, argues that many whites believed blacks could only be controlled by fear and that lynching was an effective means of control:

> . . . the fundamental cause of lynching was fear of the Negro—the basis of racism and discrimination. Many whites, after Reconstruction and during the first four decades of the twentieth century, feared that the Negro was "getting out of his place" and that the white man's social status was threatened and was in need of protection. Lynching was seen as the method to defend white domination and keep the Negroes from becoming "uppity."

We should point out that use of the term "negro" has fallen out of favor since Gibson's book was published, as has the term "colored people".

Whereas lynching occurred mostly in the South and in rural areas, race riots were occurring in the North and in urban areas during the early 20th century. As Gibson wrote in *The Negro Holocaust*, "a pattern of racial violence began to emerge in which white mob assaults were directed against entire Black communities." One such event took place in Chicago, Illinois, in 1919. The incident started when whites attempted to drive out blacks from a swimming area by throwing stones at them. One black youth, Eugene Williams, drowned after being hit in the head with a stone. Rather than arresting the white man who threw the rock, police arrested an African American, prompting a riot that lasted more than a week. In the end, 38 people were killed, 537 were injured, and at least a thousand were left homeless; most of those killed, injured, and left homeless were black.

Racial violence continues to be used to maintain racial stratification. The Federal Bureau of Investigation (FBI) has collected and published data on hate crimes since 1992. According to the FBI, an incident is determined to be a hate crime only if those investigating the incident conclude that the offender's actions were motivated purely by bias. The FBI recognizes that motivation is subjective and that it is sometimes difficult to gauge whether bias was the motivating factor of a criminal incident. Data collection also relies upon the voluntary participation and reporting practices of law enforcement agencies. Given this, we should assume that hate crimes are underreported. In 2008, the FBI reported that there were 9,691 victims (which can include persons, businesses, institutions, or society as a whole) of hate crimes. Most of the crimes reported (51 percent) were racially motivated and 13 percent were motivated by ethnicity or national origin. About 75 percent of the racially-motivated bias crimes were motivated by antiblack bias, 17 percent were motivated by antiwhite bias, and the rest involved bias toward multiracial or other racial individuals or groups.

Other examples of discrimination against racial groups often go unnoticed. One of these is the failure of institutions to provide safety or life-saving care. As recently as 2004, for example, in a report titled *Broken Promises: Evaluating the Native American Health Care System*, the U.S. Commission on Civil Rights acknowledged that "our nation's lengthy history of failing to keep its promises to Native Americans includes the failure of Congress to provide the resources necessary to create and maintain an effective health care system for Native Americans." Another example of disparate treatment seen in impoverished areas with predominantly non-white populations is the slow response times to 911 calls. Outrage over this phenomena even served as the driving force behind the lyrics of the 1990 hit song "911 is a Joke" by the outspoken, activist rap group Public Enemy.

CONSEQUENCES OF RACIAL STRATIFICATION

There are additional risks and costs (besides overt violence and violence by neglect) associated with racial stratification. Limited access to resources and power can limit access to health care, promote imprisonment, and lead to other phenomena that place individuals in direct and indirect harm. Obviously, these conditions may be more a function of income than race per se, but because race and income are so highly correlated, racial minorities suffer the consequences of living in a stratified society far more than whites do.

The risks related to racial stratification can be seen in data on **infant mortality**, or the number of babies who die at birth or by age 1 (measured as a *rate*: number per 1,000 live births). Non-Hispanic blacks have the highest infant mortality rate, almost twice that for whites. On the other end of the life cycle, black men have the lowest **life expectancy** (they live, on average, about 7 fewer years than whites). In addition, although suicide rates among African Americans are lower than those for whites, the suicide rate among black youth has been increasing far more rapidly than that for white youth. Black men are also far more likely than other groups to be murdered. According to the Centers for Disease Control, homicide is now the leading cause of death for African American men between the ages of 15 to 34. Nearly 47 percent of African American men in this age group die as a result of homicide, compared to just under 10 percent for white men.

We have already discussed the educational consequences of racial stratification, and the related sidebar provided statistical evidence that blacks and Hispanics are less likely to graduate from high school or college than whites and Asian Americans. Obviously, lower educational attainment affects employment opportunities significantly. It is no surprise then that minority group members (with the exception of Asian Americans) are more likely to be unemployed, hold low-prestige jobs, and earn lower wages than whites. According to the Bureau of Labor Statistics, for example, for every dollar earned by a white male, blacks earn about 79 cents and Hispanics about 70 cents.

Lower education and lack of job opportunities also result in higher imprisonment, which further contribute to racial stratification. Blacks, especially black men, are much more likely to spend time in prison than whites. For instance, although blacks make up approximately 13 percent of the general U.S. population, black inmates account for about 42 percent of those on death row and are far more likely to serve time in prison than other groups. Serving time in prison also lowers the chances of getting a decent job after release from prison. Indeed, research shows that, compared to whites, blacks with criminal records are less employable and earn lower wages when they do find work. Douglas Massey refers to this phenomenon as **double stigmatization**. In his 2007 work *Categorically Unequal*, Massey writes: "[In] addition to whatever burden African Americans must bear in job markets because of continued racial prejudice, a criminal record imposes a significant, *additional* social stigma."

DISCRIMINATION AGAINST WHITES?

You have undoubtedly heard people talk about reverse discrimination, or how white men are actually discriminated against while racial minorities get all the good scholarships, college acceptances, jobs, and so on. There are several important points to consider here. First, if you look back to the sidebar citing information from the National Center for Education Statistics, you'll see that whites are more likely to earn degrees than blacks and Hispanic non-whites, so this argument loses some weight. Second, it is actually illegal to use quotas or to set aside contracts for minorities unless a court has specifically ordered an organization to do so because that organization has previously been in violation of affirmative action. Third, whites are the majority possessors of power and privilege in the United States, so racial minorities have neither the financial or human capital to institutionally discriminate against whites. Finally, schools do not deliberately or numerically favor one group over another; they try to level the "playing field" so that all groups have an equal chance of success. But to whites, who are more accustomed to being in a privileged position, this very likely *feels* like discrimination.

The fact is, however, that whites enjoy a wide range of advantages, most of which are unrecognized by whites as advantages because they have always existed and are so deeply embedded within the customs and structures of society that they are taken for granted. Most whites, in fact, seldom think about or acknowledge the ways in which simply being white gives them automatic advantages or something sociologists term **white privilege**. Peggy McIntosh describes this phenomenon of white privilege as:

an invisible package of unearned assets that I can count on cashing in each day, but about which I was "meant" to remain oblivious. White privilege is like an invisible weightless knapsack of special provisions, maps, passports, codebooks, visas, clothes, tools, and blank checks.

To explore this concept, McIntosh (who is white) developed a list that includes examples of white privilege. Most white readers will easily identify with McIntosh's "knapsack"; many nonwhite readers will recognize that certain items in that knapsack are "for whites only."

White Privilege: Unpacking the Invisible Knapsack

1. I can if I wish arrange to be in the company of people of my race most of the time.

2. If I should need to move, I can be pretty sure of renting or purchasing housing in an area which I can afford and in which I would want to live.

3. I can be pretty sure that my neighbors in such a location will be neutral or pleasant to me.

4. I can go shopping alone most of the time, pretty well assured that I will not be followed or harassed.

5. I can turn on the television or open to the front page of the paper and see people of my race widely represented.

6. When I am told about our national heritage or about "civilization," I am shown that people of my color made it what it is.

7. I can be sure that my children will be given curricular materials that testify to the existence of their race.

8. If I want to, I can be pretty sure of finding a publisher for this piece on white privilege.

9. I can go into a music shop and count on finding the music of my race represented, into a supermarket and find the staple foods which fit with my cultural traditions, into a hairdresser's shop and find someone who can cut my hair.

10. Whether I use checks, credit cards or cash, I can count on my skin color not to work against the appearance of financial reliability.

11. I can arrange to protect my children most of the time from people who might not like them.

12. I can swear, or dress in second hand clothes, or not answer letters, without having people attribute these choices to the bad morals, the poverty or the illiteracy of my race.

13. I can speak in public to a powerful male group without putting my race on trial.

14. I can do well in a challenging situation without being called a credit to my race.

(continues)

(continued)

15. I am never asked to speak for all the people of my racial group.
16. I can remain oblivious of the language and customs of persons of color who constitute the world's majority without feeling in my culture any penalty for such oblivion.
17. I can criticize our government and talk about how much I fear its policies and behavior without being seen as a cultural outsider.
18. I can be pretty sure that if I ask to talk to the "person in charge," I will be facing a person of my race.
19. If a traffic cop pulls me over or if the IRS audits my tax return, I can be sure I haven't been singled out because of my race.
20. I can easily buy posters, postcards, picture books, greeting cards, dolls, toys, and children's magazines featuring people of my race.
21. I can go home from most meetings of organizations I belong to feeling somewhat tied in, rather than isolated, out-of-place, outnumbered, unheard, held at a distance, or feared.
22. I can take a job with an affirmative action employer without having my co-workers on the job suspect that I got it because of my race.
23. I can choose public accommodation without fearing that people of my race cannot get in or will be mistreated in the places I have chosen.
24. I can be sure that if I need legal or medical help, my race will not work against me.
25. I can worry about racism without being seen as self-interested or self-seeking.
26. I can chose blemish cover or bandages in "flesh" color and have them more or less match my skin.

Source: Peggy McIntosh. *White Privilege and Male Privilege*, 1988.

In sum, most sociologists believe that whites remain advantaged and privileged but acknowledge that the power dynamics are shifting. Many of the taken-for-granted advantages (such as being hired for a job because it's just assumed that the white person is more honest, hard-working, and so on) are less likely to shape everyday life in contemporary society. In other words, whites are beginning to experience what members of racial minorities have for years and it's an uncomfortable (and unfamiliar) place to be.

SUMMARY

In this chapter, we have described how racial stratification remains a part of society and how it is perpetuated at both individual and societal levels. The consequences of racial stratification are also serious and real, not just for racial minorities but for whites as well. Sociologists recognize that changing and eliminating racial stratification and inequality will be extremely difficult because individual and institutional support for this system is endemic. Ultimately change must occur on all levels, and each of us can begin by identifying ways in which we might be perpetuating racial stratification without even realizing it. By acknowledging our own contributions to the perpetuation of racial stratification we can begin to effect change.

Further Reading

American Anthropological Association. "Race: Are We So Different?" Available online at http://www.understandingrace.org/home.html. Accessed March 5, 2010.

Andersen, Margaret L., and Patricia Hill Collins. *Race, Class, and Gender: An Anthology.* Belmont, Calif.: Wadsworth Pub. Co., 2001.

Ayers, Ian. *Pervasive Prejudice? Unconventional Evidence of Race and Gender Discrimination.* Chicago: University of Chicago Press, 2001.

Bonilla-Silva, Eduardo. *Racism Without Racists: Color-blind Racism and the Persistence of Racial Inequality in the United States.* Lanham: Rowman & Littlefield Publishers, 2006.

Chou, Rosalind, and Joe R. Feagin. *The Myth of the Model Minority: Asian Americans Facing Racism.* Boulder, Colo.: Paradigm Publishers, 2008.

Gibson, Robert A. *The Negro Holocaust: Lynching and Race Riots in the United States, 1880–1950.* Yale-New Haven Teachers Institute, 1979. Available online at *http://www.yale.edu/ynhti/curriculum/units/1979/2/79.02.04.x.html*

Kozol, Jonathan. 1992. *Savage Inequalities: Children in America's Schools.* New York: HarperPerennial.

Massey, Douglas S., and Nancy A. Denton. *American Apartheid: Segregation and the Making of the Underclass.* Cambridge, Mass: Harvard University Press, 1993.

Miller, L. Scott. *An American Imperative: Accelerating Minority Educational Advancement.* New Haven: Yale University Press, 1995.

Rothenberg, Paula S. *White Privilege: Essential Readings on the Other Side of Racism.* New York: Worth Publishers, 2005.

CHAPTER 4

GENDER STRATIFICATION

INTRODUCTION

Like race and social class, gender is a social construction, and stratification on the basis of gender is the result of social arrangements, not biological factors. This is one of the most difficult concepts to get across to students because so much of our cultural conversation (or ideology) surrounding gender reinforces the idea that gender is the result of sex (biological characteristics). As you'll see in this chapter, however, inequality on the basis of gender is a function of social arrangements. In turn, gender stratification is maintained through cultural ideologies and institutional arrangements.

SEX AND GENDER

By now, it should be clear that sex and gender are not the same. **Sex**, as we commonly understand it, refers to biological and anatomical characteristics that are associated with reproductive and sexual activity. For instance, **sex hormones** (estrogen, testosterone, progesterone) play an important role in sexual development (e.g., puberty), while **anatomy** (i.e., penis, vagina, breasts) governs reproduction and sexual interactions. At an even more basic level, **sex chromosomes** (XX for female, XY for male) are genetically encoded information that determine physical and sexual development. What is interesting here is that when we think about sex differences, we often mistakenly assume that these have to do with much more than just reproduction and sexual development--but these biological factors are merely the basis and function of sex differences (in all species).

On the basis of these basic sex differences, our culture differentiates males and females. From birth (or even at the fetus stage) children are assigned a sex category—male or female. In American culture, these are the only two generally accepted categories, and infants who do not fit clearly within the male or female sex category (e.g., **intersex individuals**) may be subject to painful surgical procedures to ensure that they do fit. Interestingly, some cultures allow more flexibility in assigning sex category than we do in the U.S. by allowing for a third sex.

Once sex category is assigned, cultural expectations concerning how individuals should act, who they are, how they feel, and so on, kick in. Although as

Which Gender?

Some cultures are accepting of persons who do not fit within the 2-sex system (male or female) we understand so well in the United States. For example, the Hijra in South Asia have been recognized for centuries. These are physiological males who adopt a feminine gender role.

Hijra performance in Gujarat. *(Wikipedia. Photo by Yann Forget)*

a society we may be open to some "gender-bending," these cultural ideas and expectations are fairly universal and become associated with **gender**. Based on this interpretation, gender concerns a culture's ideas of masculinity and femininity, or what it means to be a man or a woman. Expectations associated with masculinity and femininity are learned through socialization and everyday interactions, making gender a social construction.

But although sex and gender are clearly not the same, many people assume that sex *causes* gender. That is, most people assume that biological differences between men and women (or boys and girls) dictate their behaviors and even the way their brains work. You might believe, for example, that aggression is caused by testosterone, and this explains men's more aggressive behaviors. It is true that men are more aggressive than women by almost all accounts (they commit more violent crimes, for instance) and it is also true that men, on average, have more testosterone than women. But this does not mean that testosterone causes aggression. First, it should be noted that both women and men have testosterone, and testosterone levels vary in both men and women depending upon age, genetic makeup, activity level, and other factors. Indeed, some women have higher rates of testosterone than some men. But testosterone alone does not cause aggression. The cause-effect rationale may be an inverted construct! Sociologist Michael Kimmel summarized research on the testosterone-aggression link and noted that some studies have concluded that aggression and hostility increase testosterone levels! The opposite also seems to be the case: When men are placed in nurturing roles, their testosterone levels decrease. In other words, men are not necessarily more aggressive than women because they have more male hormones (testosterone); perhaps they have more testosterone because they are more aggressive. From this perspective, it is reasonably clear that sex does not *cause* gender.

Another biological difference that is commonly assumed to cause gender differences is women's ability to bear children. From this simple reproductive/biological fact emerges a whole set of assumptions about gender differences. For instance, the idea of a "maternal instinct" suggests that women are naturally better parents than men. But this assumption ignores a wide range of evidence that suggests otherwise. Women, not men, are responsible for more cases of **infanticide**—the killing of infants. Moreover, fathers faced with raising children solo have been shown to parent just as well, and to be just as nurturing, as mothers.

Perhaps the strongest evidence that sex does not cause gender is the fact that there is considerable variation in gender across cultures. Classic research by anthropologist Margaret Mead found that in some cultures, men acted in more gentle, nurturing ways than women did, or that childcare was shared between men and women. In other cultures Mead studied, women tended to behave in ways that our culture considers more appropriate for men—competitive, aggressive, dominant, and so on. In fact, if you think about it, you can observe significant variations within our own culture in terms of gendered behaviors—some girls and women are "tomboys" and behave in traditionally masculine ways while some boys and men may be more gentle, nurturing, and emotional than many women.

Once you understand that sex does not cause gender—that is, that observed gender differences are not caused by genetics or hormones—it becomes easier to understand how gender and sex can work independently of each other. **Transgender** individuals, for instance, may embody and display gender that is different from that which we commonly associate with their biological sex. But as we mentioned earlier, it's not just transgender individuals who manifest a disconnect between sex and gender. If you think about your own life, you probably recognize times when you've displayed both "masculine" and "feminine" traits, depending upon the social context. And it is this blurring of lines in behavior that leads sociologists to believe that it is the *social context* (not our biology) that gives rise to gendered behaviors.

GENDER INEQUALITY AND DIFFERENCE

From dispelling the myth that sex causes gender, we must now move to another fundamental and important concept—that neither sex nor gender cause gender inequality. Let's consider this idea more closely. Let's suppose, for a moment, that basic biological differences between men and women lead to gender inequality. In support of this concept, you might say that men's greater size and strength translates into positions of greater power in society. Or, because women bear children, they are naturally disinclined to pursue positions in society that would afford them greater power (e.g., high-status jobs). But look more closely and you begin to see the fallacy in these suppositions.

Even if you reject the biological basis to the sex = gender = inequality argument, you might still be tempted to think that socialized differences between men and women cause power differences. Something that seems to support this premise is women "opting out" of the workforce. Much has been made of the so-called **opt-out revolution,** a trend noted by journalist Lisa Belkin, who argued that women who had achieved high-powered careers are opting out of the workforce to care for their children and homes. In connection with her observations of this trend, Belkin asks, "Why don't women run the world?" (in other words, why don't we see more women at the top of corporations and government?). Her succinct answer to this question is, "Maybe it's because they don't want to." The implication here is that women's socialization experiences lead them to care more about the well-being of their families than men do and to value paid-work less than men do. But the reality is actually quite different, according to scholars who have studied trends in women in the workforce. One thing such research has uncovered is that there really isn't a *revolution* afoot; only a small minority of women in high-earning careers leave the workforce. And those that do leave do so for reasons that are more structural than personal. That is, many leave because their jobs offer little flexibility and they find it impossible to juggle both work and family, particularly in cases where husbands were not really helping much at home, thus making the major burden of work inside and outside the home fall on women's shoulders. The bottom line here is that most of these women wanted to continue to work and would have had it been more possible. Their choices were not dictated by male vs. female personality differences and values but by the inequality built into the workplace and home/family work roles.

Indeed, Michael Kimmel and other sociologists argue that gender differences don't result in gender inequality. Instead, it's the other way around—our culture has constructed the idea of gender differences in order to justify gender inequality. Kimmel, in fact, maintains that when we really examine the evidence, we see that men and women are really not that different. If this idea seems completely ludicrous to you, stop for a moment to consider all the ways men and women are different. One common perception is "women are more emotional than men." But is that really true? To make that argument truly valid, of course, we'd have to decide how to define "emotional." If we defined it as "willing to express emotion" or even "ability to feel emotions," what we might find is that men do not express emotions as openly as women. But while it may be true that men are less likely to express emotions of vulnerability (e.g., crying or fear), this is not the same thing as saying they are less emotional. It is simply a difference in how emotion is expressed (or not expressed).

What is most important here, however, is that if society *believes* women are more emotional, this belief can have serious consequences for women's ability to succeed in social domains that have traditionally been male-dominated. One of those consequences is that they are often forced to work much harder than men to convince others that they are capable of doing the work. One sphere in which such pressure on women is prevalent is politics. Women who run for high political office, for example, must work much harder than candidates who are men in order to convince voters that they can make tough decisions and hold up under pressure.

You might be surprised to learn that most studies of gender differences (and there have been many) have found no or only small differences between men and women. In one of the most famous studies by developmental psychologists Eleanor Maccoby and Carol Jacklin reviewed over 1,600 empirical studies published over an eight year period to see whether there were significant sex differences in a wide range of behavior and attitudes. In their classic book, *The Psychology of Sex Differences*, they found only four traits for which significant evidence existed to support the claim of sex differences (verbal ability, visual/spacial ability, mathematical abilities, and aggression). In other words, for

Gender and Emotion

We are raised to believe that men and women are completely opposite from one another, especially in terms of emotionality. But research fails to support the "opposite sexes" notion. In real life, men cry and women can be tough.

(left) **Businessman cries.** *(Shutterstock);*
(above) **Hillary Clinton giving a campaign speech in Concord, New Hampshire.** *(Wikipedia. Photo by Marc Nozell)*

virtually all other abilities and traits, there was not sufficient evidence to suggest that males and females were significantly different.

Of course, there are published studies that support the idea that men and women, boys and girls, are different. But what is important to remember is that these studies also show that there is much more variation within a gender category than across gender categories. For any given behavior or trait, you'll find a great deal of variation among individuals of the same gender and this variation will be greater than that between women and men. Take the example of emotionality, discussed earlier. In concrete terms, some women (and men) are very emotional, and some women (and men) are very unemotional, with most falling between these two extremes. On average women may be somewhat more emotional than men, but this difference is not likely to be significant and certainly not enough to justify questioning any woman's ability to fight wars, run a corporation, or run for political office.

There are some important areas where gender differences do exist. At the institutional level, gender differences are undeniable. Currently, there are only

12 CEOs among the *Fortune 500* companies. Among *Fortune 1000* companies, there are only 26 women CEOs. This power differential translates into wealth. Of the 50 richest people in America, only six are women (and half of them are on the list because they inherited their fathers' wealth). At the institutional level, gender differences are very real and quite visible.

Our point here is that such differences do not arise from inherent biological or psychological differences. They are imposed upon each of us by the organizations and social interactions in which we find ourselves. Kimmel, in his book *The Gendered Society*, explains it like this:

> It would appear that the real power of gender typing resides less in the child than in the environments in which the child finds itself. The social environment is filled with gendered messages and gendered activities. Even if the child possesses no fixed and permanent gender role, social arrangements will continually reinforce gender differences. . . . Because there is considerable variation in what men and women actually do, it may require the weight of social organization and constant reinforcement to maintain gender-role differences.

In short, where gender differences might exist, sociologists would argue that they emerge because social environments impose different expectations on men and women. When situations do not call upon individuals to be "womanly" or "manly," we are likely to find women and men acting like *human* beings, not *gendered* beings.

MALE DOMINANCE

The argument that gender inequality produces gender difference assumes that gender inequality does exist. For some of you reading this volume, you might be thinking men and women are *different*, but not *unequal*, but research suggest otherwise. By virtually every measure we could use, we see that women are valued less and have less power than men. Here, we should note that we are talking about *social* differences between the genders. This is, indeed, where we are likely to see significant and consequential gender differences emerge.

One of the best collections of studies that delve into the issue of the universal devaluation of women is *Woman, Culture & Society*, a book co-authored by anthropologists Rosaldo and Lamphere. In the book, Michelle Rosaldo argues that "women may be important, powerful, and influential, but it seems that, relative to men of their age and social status, women everywhere lack generally recognized and culturally valued authority." She terms this phenomenon the **asymmetry in cultural evaluations of gender**. The idea emphasized here is that women are valued less than men, even if they perform the same role as men. Rosaldo cites many examples to support her claim. Consider just a few:

- New Guinea, where women grow sweet potatoes and men grow yams, it is the yam that is the valued food, the food that is provided at feasts.
- A Philippine society, where men hunt and women grow and harvest rice, meat is the highly valued food even though rice is the group's dietary staple.
- Australia, among aboriginal groups, men distribute meat, and meat is considered to be the best food.

What is important to recognize here is that women's role may be quite vital to the well-being of a society (few would argue with that) but they are not given as much credit as men are; the role that women perform is devalued. We can see many examples of this in our own culture. Think about the label "women's work." To say something is "women's work" is to suggest that it is trivial, unimportant, and "beneath" men.

STRATIFICATION BY GENDER

Gender stratification concerns the ways in which societal resources and rewards are distributed differently on the basis of gender. In this section, we focus on the most obvious manifestation of gender stratification: economic inequality by gender. The **gender pay gap** is one of the most persistent forms of gender inequality in the United States. Decades after passage of the **Equal Pay Act** in 1963, which was intended to equalize wages and salaries by sex for comparable jobs, women still earn considerably less than men. This gap obviously impacts economic well-being, which as we saw in Chapter 2, affects all aspects of life, from health to education.

The U.S. Department of Labor and U.S. Bureau of Labor Statistics provide data on women's and men's earnings. These agencies report that in 2009, the most recent year for which statistics are available, women who worked full-time earned on average $657 per week, whereas men earned on average $819 per week. Thus, women earn about 77 cents for every dollar men earn. The gender wage gap is not unique to the United States, but it is among the worst in the Western world. Although this gap has shrunk since 1979 when these data were first collected, it would take about 45 years (year 2057) at the current rate for the wage gap between American men and American women to disappear. As one candid blogger (C. V. Harquail) quipped, "It's possible that I won't be around in 2057. If I am around, I probably won't be lucid. And if I am lucid, I sure as hell hope that I'm not still working full time."

Considerable attention has been paid to the causes of the gender wage gap. The evidence shows that there are multiple factors involved. For instance, women are more likely than men to take time off from their jobs to raise children or care for elderly relatives, and this retards their advancement in the

Wage Gap in Selected European Countries

Country	Women's wages as % of men's
Austria	74.5
Belgium	90.9
Denmark	82.3
Finland	80
France	83.1
Germany	77
Ireland	82.9
Italy	94.9
Luxembourg	87.5
Netherlands	76.4
Portugal	91.7
Spain	82.9
Sweden	82.1
United Kingdom	78.9

Source: http://www.infoplease.com/ipa/A0908883.html

workplace as well as their income potential. Second, women tend to work at jobs that are lower paid and have limited potential for advancement, including caregiving jobs. They are also less likely to work unionized jobs, which tend to pay better than many nonunion jobs. But none of these factors can account for the gap entirely. Even when women and men work the same jobs, and the same number of hours, and are matched on other relevant employment factors, women tend to earn less.

Women are also less likely to be promoted than men. This phenomenon has been labeled the **glass ceiling effect**, particularly for women in high-powered jobs. That is, women seem to hit a "glass ceiling" on their way up—able to advance just so far. At the other end, women in lower-pay jobs such as service work, experience the **sticky floor effect**, meaning they are unable to move up from these lowest levels.

Because retirement income is based upon earnings during one's working years, the gender wage gap has lasting effects. Women receive less income from pensions than men. This is especially detrimental because women live longer than men and are therefore more likely to spend more time in old age with limited income. Indeed, elderly women are more likely to be living in poverty than elderly men.

That the gender wage gap has significant impacts on women's lives should be fairly obvious at this point. What may be less obvious is that the gap also negatively affects any men in the household as well as children. Scholars point out that in the recent economic downturn, men have been more likely than women to become unemployed. This means that many families are relying solely on the woman's job to support the family. In fact, according to research published by the Center for American Progress, more than 12 million families with children depend primarily upon the mothers' income.

But that's not the end of the story. Research by Jody Heymann also shows that women are less likely than men to have paid leave (even though women are much more likely to be responsible for caretaking), and fewer choices about when to start and end their workdays than men. According to Heymann, "On all measures of job autonomy (such as having a say on what jobs are to be done), women had less flexibility and decision-making authority than men."

HOW GENDER STRATIFICATION IS MAINTAINED
Organizational/Institutional Forces

In recent years, gender scholars have explored **gendered organizations**—organizations with norms and practices that are based on and mirror masculine norms and practices. As Joan Acker posits in her article entitled "Hierarchies, jobs, bodies: A theory of gendered organizations":

> To say that an organization . . . is gendered means that advantage and disadvantage, exploitation and control, action and emotion, meaning and identity, are patterned through and in terms of a distinction between male and female, masculine and feminine.

Acker argues that one of the ways organizations are gendered is through segregating division of labor, allowed behaviors, physical spaces, and so on, along gendered lines. For example, men tend to be managers and women work as their assistants; important business decisions may be made in settings where women are not likely to be present such as the golf course, the men's room, or over cocktails after work. Yale University professor Victoria Brescoll also found that women who express anger in the workplace are judged more harshly than are men; men can be "bossy" without having their masculinity called into question but if women are bossy (even when they are the boss) they are perceived as being "too bossy" and worse.

The idea that organizations are gendered may seem difficult to understand because we are raised to believe that organizations are fair, rational, and gender-neutral. We may assume that companies want to hire the best workers, regardless of their gender (or race, or other irrelevant attribute). The problem is that those who define the "best worker" (especially when it comes to male-dominant jobs that, coincidentally, pay better than female-dominant jobs) are men. Moreover, the requirements for the job in question are defined in masculine ways, even though the defining may be more subtle than overt. One interesting way that certain jobs are a "better fit" for men is explained by Joan Williams, author of *Unbending Gender*. Williams notes that equipment (or even furnishings) in these traditionally male jobs fit men's bodies better than women's. As an example, Williams cites the "cockpit case," where the courts ruled that airline cockpits are designed so that they are better fit for men's bodies than women's, thereby disqualifying more women pilots than men pilots.

Let's consider another way in which organizations structure the lives of men and women differently and as a result, end up rewarding them differently. Research shows that parenthood is not treated the same within organizations for women and men. Men benefit income-wise when they become parents; women do not. In fact, many organizations wittingly or unwittingly institute a **fatherhood bonus** and a **motherhood penalty**. Sociologists Melissa Hodges and Michelle Budig found that even after one takes into account factors such as marital status, number of hours worked, and so on, fathers earn more than childless men. For mothers, incomes dropped by about 7 percent per child. By

Studies show that a woman's pay declines with each child, whereas a man's pay tends to increase when he becomes a father. *(Wikipedia. Photo by Eric Ward)*

the way, Hodges and Budig found that the fatherhood bonus was greatest for white men, and that black men did not enjoy as great a boost in their earnings—another example of how race and gender can interact to produce different experiences among persons of different groups.

Another strongly gendered institution is the family. As sociologists have long recognized, virtually every aspect of family life is structured along gendered lines. This may seem strange to think about because the contemporary marriage ideal is **egalitarianism**, with most people believing that men and women should be equal in marriage and preferring a marriage where husbands and wives are partners. But ideals do not always match reality.

Other studies show that although most women work outside the home, many in full-time jobs, men have really not changed the amount of work they do within the home. Recent research, for example, shows that the gap between how much time women and men spend doing housework has shrunk over the past few decades, but that's mostly because women are doing *less* housework, not that men are doing substantially *more*. In other words, housework remains very gendered. Not only do

Coverture

In earlier centuries, women in the United States (and elsewhere) became the property of men upon entering into a marriage contract. This practice was facilitated in the United States through a common law rule called **coverture**. Per the doctrine of coverture, a woman's identity was superseded by that of her husband, a construct that reduced a married woman to property or **chattel**. Religion played a major role in supporting this prac-

A pair of wedding rings. *(Wikipedia. Photo by Jeff Belmonte)*

tice. Religious traditionalists emphasized the literal meaning of biblical teachings, and therefore supported male domination in marital relationships. Secular changes in the past century have brought about a new sense of marriage equality—and a new sense of general equality on the basis of gender. Although forms of gender discrimination such as coverture may seem like ancient ideals buried by decades of legal precedence and common practice, as recently as 1998, members of the Southern Baptist Church were calling for women to "submit graciously to the leadership of their husbands."

women do more housework than men, the types of housework they do differs from men's. Women are more likely to do tasks essential to day-to-day functioning of the family (e.g., cooking, caring for children), whereas men's tasks are more sporadic (e.g., mowing the lawn, doing handy work).

One area where men's participation in home-life has increased (though still does not equal women's) is childcare. Sociologist Suzanne Bianchi and her colleagues have studied changes in men's participation in childcare over time. They compared the amount of time fathers spent with their children over several decades (from the 1960s to the 2000s) and found that today's fathers have nearly tripled the amount of time they spend with children. On average, today's fathers spend about seven hours per week with children. Interestingly, with one exception, that timeframe does not vary significantly whether their wives work outside of the home or not. That exception has to do with active "minding" of children, which engages fathers with employed wives more than fathers with stay-at-home wives.

This gender gap in labor within the home reflects what we call the **second shift**. The second shift was a term coined by Arlie Hochschild, who found that women in effect had two full-time jobs—the first in the workplace, the second in the home. Some scholars have even identified a **third shift**, which alludes to the additional labor of worrying about the children, the home, work, and all the other demands on women's busy lives. Certainly men have hectic lives, but Michele Bolton, author of *The Third Shift*, suggests that few men experience the same level of anxiety and psychological angst that women do.

Earlier we discussed how anthropologists find that women's work throughout the world is valued less than men's. This is certainly true for caregiving (e.g., childcare, health care work), which is typically performed by women. Individuals who perform caregiving for pay earn significantly less than those in comparable jobs that do not involve caregiving. According to the U.S. Bureau of Labor Statistics, full-time childcare providers earn less than garbage collectors and gas station employees.

It should be rather obvious by now that organizations and institutions are gendered and that these gendered institutions are one of the major reasons gender stratification persists. If women are primarily responsible for childcare and housework, they have less time to devote to their jobs, especially jobs that require long hours, and their incomes may suffer as a result. In the end, they have access to less money, power, and authority—and this is the very basis or definition of gender stratification.

Cultural Ideologies

There are many ways that cultural practices and ideologies support gender stratification. One of the most important ideologies is associated with what we call **separate spheres**, the separation between work and home that began in the late 1700s with the Industrial Revolution. Prior to this, families were the site of production or work. Moreover, before work was separated from the home, men and women worked cooperatively to maintain the household. Women farmed alongside their husbands, and men taught their sons their craft.

After the Industrial Revolution, work moved into factories, and families became consumption units rather units of production. Thus, "family" and "work" were delegated to separate spheres. Under this new arrangement, women were seen as primarily responsible for the home, whereas men were responsible for earning a wage. The ideology that grew out of this separation was that the home was the natural place for women, whereas men's natural role was outside the home. Women's primary role centered on domesticity, men's on public service. An important aspect of this division was that women also assumed the role of emotional caretaker of the family. It was their responsibility to see to it that husbands and children were emotionally satisfied and fulfilled.

Although separate spheres are no longer status quo for most American families—the majority of married women and men work outside the home—the ideology behind this social construct has lingered. For instance, 37 percent of Americans still agree that it is better for a man to work outside the home and for a woman to tend to the home. This ideology explains, in part, why men continue to do less housework than women, even when their wives work full time. It probably also explains why women are still viewed as better emotional caretakers.

Another cultural belief that serves to maintain gender stratification is the belief in the existence of pervasive and widespread gender differences, or the belief that men and women are completely opposite biologically and psychologically. Recall our earlier argument that this ideology is not supported by empirical research because differences that do emerge tend to be relatively small and suggest that there is more variation within groups than between groups.

So if there are no significant gender differences in personality, why do we perpetuate the idea that there are? Why, in fact, are men and women viewed as polar or planetary opposites, to use Michael Kimmel's metaphor? We return to the point we raised earlier—that the function of gender difference is to legitimize and justify inequality. Just imagine for a moment that there really are no significant or meaningful personality differences between men and women. If this were universally accepted, what justification could possibly exist for paying women less or burdening them with housework?

There are many other gender-related ideologies we could discuss, but the point is that all of these serve to reinforce gender stratification and inequality. The lingering separate spheres ideology means that women feel primarily responsible for caring for the home, and as a result, can devote less time to other pursuits, including leisure (Arlie Hochschild estimated that compared to men, women work an extra month of 24-hour days each year). And as long as we believe gender differences at the individual level are real and meaningful, then differential treatment of men and women can be justified. Furthermore, if we believe that gender differences are real, and not social constructions or ideologies, we might conclude that there's no reason to question or fight for change because nothing would change anyway.

Interpersonal and Personal Interaction

One of the major ways in which gender inequality is sustained in daily life is through social interaction. There are expectations for behavior associated with gender, and we all—through the gender socialization process—learn what these are. Thus, in many ways, every day, most people reinforce gender roles. How one dresses, speaks, walks, looks at others, and so on, can be said to be gendered. Obviously, everyone has the option to dress in gender-neutral or other-gender garb—but most people do not. For most people, their sense of who they are as men or women—their gender identity—is deeply felt and they *embody* these identities in the way they dress and act.

Sociologists have coined the phrase **doing gender** to suggest that we continually display and accomplish our gender through social interaction. As sociologist Sara Crawley and her colleagues assert: "If gender is not innate, how is it possible that most people conform to the standards? Simple: we are called upon to perform according to gender expectations—gender is a social performance of the body."

We all "do gender" on a daily basis, even if we're not aware of doing so. And although these gender performances reinforce larger gender structures, it should be recognized that most people enjoy playing out their gender roles. Indeed, because gender identities are so deeply ingrained, and because society reinforces appropriate gender behavior at every turn, it feels comfortable and enjoyable to enact our roles. If you identify as masculine, recall a time when you were asked to change a flat tire for a woman (and could do so); if you identify as feminine, recall a time when you felt sexy and attractive. The masculine person doesn't necessarily enjoy getting dirty, but there is unquestionably a satisfaction in feeling "manly." The feminine individual doesn't necessarily dress for others or expect the appreciative remark, but it can feel good to have one's femininity affirmed in this way. Barbara Risman, in her book *Gender Vertigo*, calls this **gendered play**. She notes in particular that most people enjoy playing with their appearance (clothes, makeup, looks) and that one reason people are afraid of changing gender structures is that we may have to give up the fun of being "girly" or "manly." In her words: "My guess is that at least some of the deeply felt reaction to changing gendered roles . . . springs from the fear of going too far, of denying one of the few means of easily accessible, social acceptable, nonfattening, healthy pleasures available to us: doing gender in ways we enjoy."

At the same time, Risman recognizes that "we cannot have inequality unless we have difference." By "doing gender," we reaffirm our own sense of ourselves as gendered beings and reinforce others' perceptions of gender as an essential aspect of the social world. And this sense of difference justifies differential treatment (inequality). In this way, interpersonal interactions play a major role in maintaining gender stratification.

CONSEQUENCES OF GENDER STRATIFICATION

We have already discussed two of the most important consequences of gender stratification—the wage gap and the second shift. Here we discuss another important and devastating consequence of gender stratification—violence against women. Although there are multiple explanations for violence against women, gender inequality is generally recognized as an important cause. The devaluation of women in general, makes it more likely that they will be targeted for abuse. Women's more limited economic resources make it harder to escape violent relationships once they begin.

According to the Centers for Disease Control and Prevention (CDC) women experience two million injuries annually from **intimate partner violence** (IPV), 600,000 of which require medical attention. It is important to note that women are not the *only* victims of **domestic violence** (DV) or IPV. But although men can be victims of IPV, the most common form of DV or IPV includes a male perpetrator and a female victim. According to the Bureau of Justice Statistics, intimate partners are responsible for 26 percent of all violence against women and just 5 percent of violence against men.

Rape and sexual assault are crimes committed almost entirely against women and girls. According to the U.S. Bureau of Justice Statistics, in 2007, there were about 11,300 rapes or sexual assaults of men and 236,980 of women. Contrary to the belief that rape is committed by strangers, most rape victims know their rapists. For example, among college women who are raped, 90 percent knew their attackers. For many women and girls, just the fear of rape keeps them from walking alone at night, going to a club or party alone, feeling completely safe when home alone, working jobs that will put them in certain parts of town or at hours of the day that are deemed unsafe, and so on.

Not only is violence, and especially sexual assault, an *outcome* of gender inequality, it also *reinforces* gender inequality. Violence is a form of social control of women, a way to remind them that they do not belong in certain jobs or cannot fully enjoy public domain. The obvious example of this is **sexual harassment,** which according to the Equal Employment Opportunity Commission (EEOC) involves "*unwelcome* sexual advances, requests for sexual favors, and other verbal or physical conduct of a sexual nature," (emphasis added). One recent study of U.S. workers found that 31 percent of women had been harassed in their jobs, compared to 7 percent of men. All of the women had been harassed

Defining Sexual Harassment in the Courts

In the 1970s, following the advent of Affirmative Action programs, formerly male-dominated professions were legally required to integrate women into their workforces for the first time. Lois Jenson was among the first women hired by Eveleth, an iron mine located in Northern Minnesota. Jenson and the other women miners endured extreme sexual harassment that included sexual advances, verbal threats, and other maltreatment. Because she was afraid of losing her job, Jenson remained quiet until the harassment became intolerable. She then faced further discrimination as the company and various agencies failed to respond to her grievances and complaints. Eventually, after enduring three trials and more than 10 years of setbacks and disappointment, Jenson and the other women miners won their case and comprised the plaintiffs in the first class-action lawsuit filed on the basis of sexual harassment in the U.S.

Men sometimes face sexual harassment as well—typically at the hands of other men. The pivotal case that exhibited how sexual harassment can exist among members of the same sex is *Oncale v. Sundowner.* Mr. Oncale was part of an eight-man (all heterosexual) crew on an oil platform in the Gulf of Mexico. Over the period of his employment, Oncale was subjected to humiliation, which included being grabbed and having his co-workers remove their pants while threatening to have sex with him. On one occasion, while he was showering, some of the men sexually abused him with a bar of soap. Upon resigning, Mr. Oncale filed a complaint of sexual harassment, which was rejected on the grounds that same-sex harassment was not a valid concern. The U.S. Supreme Court disagreed with the lower court's ruling and eventually established a precedent that sexual intentions are not a prerequisite for sexual harassment and that sexual harassment applies to same-sex relationships as well as to opposite-sex relationships.

Source: http://www.sexualharassmentsupport.org/SHworkplace.html

by men, as had 41 percent of the male victims. While sexual harassment occurs in all types of jobs, women who work in jobs that have traditionally been male dominant (e.g., women who work as police officers, autoworkers, fire fighters) are at greater risk of being sexually harassed.

SUMMARY

This chapter focused on the ways that gender stratification operates in everyday life. In the words of Barbara Risman, gender is "built in to social life via socialization, interaction, and institutional organizations." Because gender is so ingrained in our culture and occupies a central place at both micro and macro levels of society, many scholars argue that it is one of the hardest forms of inequality to fight. This may be especially true because gender differences seem so normal and natural—not the social constructions that we have argued them to be in this chapter. But once you understand that gender inequality is based on the *belief* (not reality) of gender difference, it becomes harder to overlook or ignore all the ways, subtle and not so subtle, that gender inequality occurs in daily life.

What a world without gender differences, and hence gender inequality, might look like is open for debate. For most of us, the idea of "sameness" or **androgyny**—being neither feminine nor masculine—is unappealing. But as Michael Kimmel points out, people commonly mistake "equality for sameness." Kimmel argues that what is needed is not a neutralizing of gender, but a redefinition of masculinity and femininity. The change Kimmel calls for is not for men and women to become more similar but for men and women to become more equal, and for those behaviors and traits associated with masculinity and femininity to be labeled as *human* traits and behaviors rather than exclusively men's or women's traits. We end here with a poignant quotation from Kimmel's *The Gendered Society*, which offers a glimpse of what this might look like:

> Love, tenderness, nurturance; competence, ambition, assertion—these are human qualities, and all human beings—both women and men—should have equal access to them. And when we do express them, we are expressing, respectively, our gender identities, not the gender of the other. What a strange notion, indeed, that such emotions should be labeled as masculine or feminine, when they are so deeply human and when both women and men are so easily capable of a so much fuller range of feelings.

Further Reading

Bolton, Michele. *The Third Shift: Managing Hard Choices in Our Careers, Homes, and Lives as Women.* San Francisco: Jossey-Bass, 2000.

Crawley, Sara L., Lara J. Foley, and Constance L. Shehan. *Gendering Bodies.* Lanham: Rowman & Littlefield Publishers, 2008.

Gordon, Margaret T., and Stephanie Riger. *The Female Fear.* New York: The Free Press, 1989.

Heymann, Jody. *The Widening Gap: Why America's Working Families Are in Jeopardy and What Can Be Done About It.* N.Y: Basic Books, 2000.

Hochschild, Arlie Russell, with Anne Machung. *The Second Shift.* New York: Avon Books, 1989.

Kimmel, Michael. *The Gendered Society.* 3rd ed. NewYork: Oxford University Press, 2008.

Lorber, Judith. *Breaking the Bowls: Degendering and Feminist Change.* New York: W.W. Norton & Co, 2005.

Risman, Barbara J. *Gender Vertigo: American Families in Transition.* New Haven: Yale University Press, 1998.

Rosaldo, Michelle Zimbalist, and Louise Lamphere (Eds.) *Woman, Culture & Society.* Stanford, Calif.: Stanford University Press, 1974.

Stone, Pamela. *Opting Out? Why Women Really Quit Careers and Head Home.* Berkeley, Calif.: University of California Press, 2007.

Tanenbaum, Leora. *Slut! Growing Up Female with a Bad Reputation.* New York: Perennial, 2000.

CHAPTER 5

STRATIFICATION OF ANIMALS AND CHILDREN

It might seem strange to include a chapter on children and animals in a book about stratification, and especially to include them together in the same chapter. What do animals and children have in common? For that matter, doesn't **stratification**, or the system by which societies organize themselves and determine the distribution of resources, apply only to humans? And if we think about the implications of stratification in terms of mistreatment or discrimination, you might wonder what that has to do with children and animals. Animals and children are adored, right? Indeed, we often hear people say that children are our most precious resources, and pets are practically "family."

But sociologists look beyond what people say about certain groups and look closely at how these groups are actually treated in society. For instance, are they afforded the same resources as others? Are they more or less vulnerable to abuses of power? Are there conflicting **ideologies**, or widespread cultural beliefs, about these groups? In other words, can animals and children be both loved and even adored, yet powerless and denigrated? Answers to these questions reveal that children and animals are indeed part of the social stratification system, and arguably, at the bottom.

This chapter, in fact, is about two groups in society that have virtually no "voice," literally or figuratively. For the most part, neither children nor animals are perceived to have many rights, and by and large, this situation is considered natural and acceptable. Despite the fact that they often cannot voice their complaints or are not taken seriously when they do, it is important to consider their conditions in order to more fully understand power, exploitation, and inequality in society. This, after all, is the crux of social stratification.

SOCIOLOGICAL PERSPECTIVES ON CHILDREN AND ANIMALS

Sociological interest in animals and in children is relatively new. Traditionally, sociological discussions of stratification have ignored these two groups altogether. It is interesting to note, for example, that when sociologists discuss the concept of **ageism**—discrimination on the basis of age—they refer almost exclusively to discrimination against older persons. In fact, there isn't a word to describe discrimination against very young people. This gap in the language is more than just an oversight—it is reflective of how children, and the study of childhood, are perceived as less important than others in sociological studies of stratification. This lack of attention to children is one of many clues about their relative powerlessness and low status in society at large.

Although there is a word to describe discrimination against animals (**speciesism**), nonhuman animals are perceived as occupying a much lower position than humans. Very few people would argue that animals share the same rights that humans have, such as rights to autonomy, privacy, and self-determination. Even though animals play an important role in humans' lives (as pets or as a food source) and occupy a central role in our cultural imaginations (think Mickey Mouse or *Ice Age*), sociologists have virtually ignored the human–animal connection. Instead, sociology is a very **anthropocentric** discipline in that it focuses almost exclusively on humans. When sociologists do turn their attention to animals, it is often to reassert the superiority of humans over all other species. One of the most famous sociologists, George Herbert Mead, wrote a book entitled *Mind, Self, and Society,* a classic text about how individuals become a part of a culture. Mead argued that humans had unique capacities and that only humans can create culture and language, a point that has been challenged more recently by research on primate behavior and animal psychology.

So although the focus of sociology is always on humans, and usually on adults, examination of the ways in which humans interact with children and animals provides a window through which we can view stratification in a more holistic way. Both groups provide important insight into oppressive and exploitative practices within society and humans' participation in these activities. Because much of the oppression and exploitation of children and animals is viewed as normal, these practices also tell us a lot about the functions of stratification in society.

CULTURAL PERCEPTIONS AND TREATMENT OF CHILDREN AND ANIMALS

There are interesting similarities in how we treat and think about children and animals, especially domesticated animals. Both children's and domesticated

How Different Are Animals and Humans?

Until recently, it was simply *known* that humans were superior to animals. The prevailing view was that humans used conscious thought, animals used instinct; humans laughed, animals didn't; humans used tools, animals didn't; humans developed social communities, animals did not; humans used language, animals did not have such capacity; and so on and so on. Recent research has challenged these commonsense notions. Consider the following:

- Azy (orangutan) communicates through abstract symbols on a computer screen and has shown that he can understand another individual's perspective, a capability scientists call theory of mind.
- Kanzi (bonobo) uses lexigrams to communicate, understands spoken English, and makes and uses stone tools.
- Koko (gorilla) communicates using American Sign Language.
- Momo (marmoset) learns through imitation and has a sense of object permanence—the knowledge that something out of sight still exists.
- Aristides (ring-tailed lemur) can repeat arbitrary sequences on a computer screen and discriminate between quantities.
- Alex (African gray parrot) counted, identified shapes and colors, and understood the concept of same and different.
- Psychobird (western scrub jay) recalls the past, plans for the future, and understands the concept of deceptive behavior.
- Uek and Betty (New Caledonian crows) can solve problems and use tools.
- Dolphins understand grammar and syntax, show self-awareness, are creative, and recognize that instructions given on a television screen are representations of the real world.
- Betsy and Rico (border collies) understand hundreds of words and the objects they represent.
- Elephants have been shown to exhibit self-awareness and have long memories.
- Sheep can recognize individual faces—human and sheep—and retain the recognition long term.
- Octopi use tools, exhibit play behavior, recognize individuals, and have distinct personalities.
- African cichlids determine social ranking through observation, and exhibit signs of logical reasoning.

Source: National Geographic Magazine. March 2008.

animals' physical bodies are closely monitored and controlled. When you think about it, almost all aspects of children's physical existence—where they play, learn, eat, relax—are controlled and monitored by adults. Even basic bodily functions such as eating and elimination—are closely supervised, especially for very young children. Children today spend far less time without adult supervision than they did in the past. Even when children are allowed free time to play or interact with friends without the constraints of adult supervision, their ability to determine where and how long to interact is usually restricted. This is especially true for children in middle-class and upper-class families. This close monitoring of children has been the result of increased concerns about children's potential victimization.

Some domesticated animals (especially predators such as dogs and cats) possess considerable physical strength but their bodies (like children's) are monitored, restrained, and controlled. For instance, many domesticated cats are declawed, a procedure that removes their primary defense mechanism. Most communities have strict codes requiring that dogs be leashed, and stray dogs are captured and caged. Many domesticated animals as well as animals living in zoos are physically confined, their schedules regimented, and their bodily functions monitored. Both children and animals also are perceived by adults to require extensive training and socialization. The desired result, of course, is to make their behavior more acceptable for those in power (adults).

Thus, on a physical level, children's and animals' lives are strikingly similar. There are other similarities as well. Both children and animals lack certain rights that we afford adults. Although there are laws preventing cruelty against children and animals, it is legal in the United States to use corporal (physical) punishment on animals and children even though these two groups are least able to defend themselves against violence or escape from it.

Most importantly, animals and children are among the few beings who cannot advocate for themselves in cases of injustice. Obviously, animals cannot do so because they literally cannot speak for themselves. Our legal system is designed to ensure *human* rights, so animals rarely are the subject of any legal action (although their owners may be if they fail to control their animals). Children possess the linguistic capacity to speak, but beliefs about children's inability to express informed opinions means that they are not allowed to vote, work until approaching legal adulthood, or make decisions about marriage or living arrangements without adult consent. In this way, both animals and children lack legal say or "voice." When children's concerns do need to be heard in the legal system, courts will often appoint child advocates to speak for children (even those who may be able to speak coherently for themselves).

If one examines media portrayals of children or animals, you will also see that both are used extensively in advertisements and other media offerings. Both are considered to have a high "cute factor" and as such, are used extensively to sell products. Indeed, there is a tendency to "cutify" animals in order to sell products, including the animals' own meat. In fact, a common strategy in advertisements is to present animals in childlike ways, a practice known as **neoteny**, which focuses on retaining and emphasizing youthful, childlike features in adult forms (human or animal). Think of Mickey Mouse, for instance. Mickey has a large round face, large eyes, and small limbs. These are neotenized, or childlike, features that are used to represent animals in the public eye. Making animals more childlike enables humans to maintain a greater power over them. As Daniel Harris argues in his book *Cute, Quaint, Hungry and Romantic: The Aesthetics of Consumerism*, when objects are made "cute," they are disempowered and appear more vulnerable and ignorant than they in fact are. This is one way media reflects and reinforces social inequalities.

As you will see in this chapter, animals and children are *defined* by those in power (adult humans). Rather than seeing *animals* or *children* as they are, adults often project their own expectations and ideas onto these less powerful groups.

ANIMALS IN SOCIETIES

Humans have had a long and complex relationship with nonhuman animals, dating back thousands of years. Some of the temples in Egypt contain mummified cats which suggests that they were domesticated more than 5,000 years ago. Today, virtually everyone interacts or engages with nonhuman animals on a regular basis—as pets, workers, or food. Many of these relationships are based on genuine love and compassion, others are not.

Animals as Companions

Nearly two out of every three households in the United States have pets. Many families consider their furry, feathered, or scaly friends to be *family* and celebrate their pets' birthdays and holidays with special gifts just as they would with their own children. Annual expenditures for pets in the United States exceed $45 billion, according to the American Pet Products Association, Inc. Further evidence of just how important pets are to humans can be found in the increasing number of divorces that involve prolonged and ugly custody battles—not over who gets the children but who gets Fido or Tiger when couples split. And it's not just household pets that we love. Americans also love whales, birds, elephants, and other wild animals, and spend billions on wildlife conservation each year.

Households with children are most likely to have pets. Many parents believe that pets teach children important life lessons like responsibility, empathy, and the cycle of life. Indeed, many children's first experience with death comes from having a beloved pet die. Such experiences can teach children about life and death and help them deal with the grief they face when confronted with the deaths of grandparents and other relatives.

Research shows that children's relationships with pets are often very close. Many children consider their pets to be among their best friends and turn to them when they are sad, angry, hurt or lonely. Pets can ease children's anxieties and provide important social support. Purdue University researcher Gail Melson maintains that pets play an important role in children's development in other ways as well. Babies find animals appealing to look at, touch, hear and

Pets teach children responsibility, nurturing, and about life and death. *(Library of Congress)*

interact with, and these reactions can stimulate infants' and toddlers' learning, attention and curiosity.

Individuals of all ages benefit from animal companionship. Indeed, one of the most important developments in health care is the introduction of companion animals for therapeutic purposes and to assist persons with special needs (e.g., blindness, epilepsy). Therapy animals have been introduced into nursing homes, schools, psychiatric institutions, even prisons. Animals in these settings have been shown to facilitate the mental, physical, and emotional growth and well-being for many individuals.

Animals as Subordinates

People often view animals in very fond terms and develop close relationships with them. But an important aspect to these human–animals relationships is that animals are expected to satisfy humans' needs, not the other way around. Often this includes the human need for companionship and affection. Animals are also frequently used to facilitate some type of human task or labor. Farm animals, for example, are raised primarily to provide food for humans. Animals are used in science laboratories to test the safety of drugs and chemicals for human use. Animal skins and furs are used for fashion. Even bringing a pet into the family to help children learn empathy or responsibility can be seen as a way human parents employ animals to assist them in socializing children.

Even though animals gain some benefits from their relationships with humans, humans rarely connect with animals as *animals*. Instead, people seek to control animals' behaviors in an attempt to make them conform to human expectations. When animals *do* act like animals, as when circus animals attack their trainers or dogs or primates kill or maim their owners, there is usually a sense of shock—not just because of the horrific or tragic nature of these situations or the injuries sustained by the humans involved, but because we are perplexed that animals actually "turned on" their trainer or owner. So accustomed are we to seeing animals "behave" in ways humans deem appropriate that we may fail to recognize or consider that animals' true natures can be quite different from those we've projected onto them.

Humans have a tendency to ascribe many human attributes to animals, rather than relating to them as animals. This tendency is called **anthropomorphism**. Popular movies such as *Shrek* or *Ice Age*, books such as *Alice in Wonderland*, and a whole host of fairy tales (such as *Cinderella*) portray animals with human emotions, motives, and attributes. But anthropomorphism does not just come from Hollywood; it can be seen next door. Have you ever, for example, seen people dress their pets up in fancy outfits? This is a classic case of anthropomorphism. And although it seems cute and innocent, it is another example of how humans seek to re-create animals in their own image and fail to relate to pets as nonhuman animals.

Dressing animals up in human clothing distances people from animals' true natures and allows humans to more easily project their own desires, needs, and expectations onto their pets. *(Wikipedia. Photo by Randy Robertson)*

Keep in mind too that all subjugated groups are defined by those in power. Those groups and individuals in society with the highest status have the power to "define" others—that is, to shape people's perceptions and attitudes about the subordinate group. Whenever humans create animals in their own image (through anthropomorphism), they are exercising power over the other. It is also important to recognize that the group being defined need not realize that such definitions have been imposed. That is, just because animals do not understand that (or how) humans have defined or subjugated them does not mean that subordination has not occurred.

Even the language surrounding pet ownership and animal–human relationships suggest a strong dominant–subordinate relationship. The human owner is the "master." Pets must be "trained." Humans are said to have "dominion" (control, rule, dominance) over animals. Such language leaves little doubt that people believe they are superior to animals—intellectually, emotionally, and spiritually.

Oppression of Animals

People love their animals, and animals and people both benefit from connections formed over thousands of years. But the human–animal connection also has a dark side. Though deeply loved, animals are also the most oppressed group in society. As such, they are subject to abuse, exploitation, and denigration.

The belief system concerning nonhuman animals that serves as the basis of their oppression is called **speciesism**, the belief in the inherent superiority of humans over other animals. This belief assigns greater value to humans than to other animals. Speciesist beliefs clearly designate nonhuman animals as the "other." Within this system, animals are viewed as inferior to humans and valued only for what they can provide to humans. The widespread belief that animals were placed on earth to provide food for humans, for example, is rooted in speciesism. Taken to an extreme, speciesism can be used to justify the killing and abuse of animals.

Not all cultures share these beliefs. Native American cultures, for example, display a great reverence for animals and strive to maintain harmonious rather than exploitive relationships with animals. Respect for all beings, including animals, is written into their 10 commandments. Vegans also believe that no animal should be used for entertainment purposes or eaten. For some vegans, this includes not eating honey because it is produced by bees and not wearing leather since it comes from cows. The fact that perceptions of and beliefs about animals vary so greatly across groups or cultures suggests that beliefs in the inherent superior of humans is a social construction and not a natural condition. As such, it is a subject meriting sociological investigation.

Animal Cruelty and Abuse

Although all states in the United States have animal cruelty laws, there are no standard definitions, and what constitutes abuse differs from state to state. In Delaware, a person is guilty of animal cruelty if he or she "Intentionally or recklessly subjects an animal to cruel mistreatment, cruel neglect, kills or injures an animal without the owner's consent, cruelly or unnecessarily kills or injures any animal." In Georgia, animal cruelty is defined as an action that "causes death or unjustifiable physical pain or suffering to any animal by an act, an omission, or willful neglect. Willful neglect means the intentional withholding of food and water required by an animal to prevent starvation or dehydration." In many states, exceptions are made for such things as farming, animal training, research, hunting, or veterinary practices. In Alabama, exceptions are made for "shooting a dog or cat for urinating or defecating on property."

Because definitions of and punishments for cruelty to animals vary widely, it is difficult to determine the prevalence of animal abuse. There are databases, however, that attempt to track instances reported to authorities. More than 15,000 cases are currently posted on the Animal Abuse Crime Database. Certainly this is an underestimate because most cases are never reported.

Abuse of animals is not limited to certain groups or types of people. In fact, one of the most famous cases involved Michael Vick, formerly a star quarterback for the Atlanta Falcons and one of the richest athletes in the world (estimated annual income over $25 million). In 2007, police discovered that Vick was involved in an interstate dog fighting ring, a "sport" deemed illegal due to its viciousness and cruelty. In addition to witnessing and supporting dog fights, Vick admitted to hanging or drowning dogs that did not perform well in the fights. Vick was sentenced to serve nearly two years in federal prison for the crime.

Almost everyone who read accounts of Vick's behavior was appalled by the cruelty directed at the dogs and defined his actions as animal abuse. Indeed, the public outcry against Vick was intense. Yet other forms of animal cruelty go largely unheeded. According to Erik Marcus, author of *Meat Market*, animals bred in **concentrated animal feeding operations** (CAFOs) are subjected to horrific practices: Chicks' beaks are seared; cattle are castrated, dehorned, branded and have their tails docked—all without anesthesia. Nor are animals necessarily dead before their throats are cut or they are scalded to remove feathers. Animal abuse also exists in the entertainment industry. To train circus animals to perform unnatural tricks, trainers use electric shocks, hooks, whips, and ropes in ways that—if inflicted on a pet by you or me—would be illegal in just about every state.

An important lesson about stratification is that those individuals who are more powerful can and do define actions in ways that will benefit them. Thus, as noted above, laws concerning animal cruelty typically exclude actions associated with such things as farming, hunting, and animal training. Because powerful corporations, industries and organizations are primarily responsible for operating CAFOs, circuses, and the like, these actions are perceived as legitimate and even necessary. There are few powerful enough to challenge such practices—certainly not the animals themselves.

The Link Between Animal Abuse and Other Violence

One of the primary interests sociologists have in animal abuse is in understanding the connection between animal abuse and other forms of violence. In households where violence against children or a spouse is exercised, it is common for pets to be physically threatened and abused as well. Studies also show a strong association between children's cruelty towards animals and later criminal behavior. For the most part, adults who commit violent crimes report higher rates of animal abuse as children. One might assume that these cases involve sadistic children who grow up to be sadistic adults. But recent research suggests that children growing up in abusive households are sometimes enticed into abusing animals by the abuser. For instance, Dana Atwood-Harvey found that children sometimes abuse animals as a way to protect their pets from worse harm from an abusive adult or because they are forced to do so by an abuser. In her article entitled "From touchstone to tombstone: Children's experiences with the abuse of their beloved pets," Atwood-Harvey recalls her own experience as a child:

> Patches, Spot, and I were outside playing ball. Patches was at my side and Spot was across the yard, ball in mouth. My father came storming outside. Just hearing the door slam, we all stopped mid-play. Spot dropped the ball and raced to my side. My father was screaming that the neighbor had called about the dogs getting in his garbage. As my Dad stormed across the lawn, all three of us huddled together in the grass. Patches was quivering in my arms and Spot was whining as he stood in front of us. . . . As he screamed at us with fists clenched, I kept thinking that he was going to kill them. Finally, when he reached down to pull me away, I turned on the dogs myself. I stood up quickly and started screaming at the dogs, "You naughty dogs!" Then, I started pounding on them with my fists as I repeated "naughty dogs, bad dogs." I never even heard my father go back into the house through the yelps and cries of my most cherished companions. All I know was that when I stopped, he was gone. When I noticed that my father was gone, I lay down in the grass and sobbed.

Animals factor into abusive relationships in other important ways. Amy Fitzgerald has studied the relationship between victims of abuse and their pets. She found that animals help victims cope with the abuse and even keep women from taking their own lives to escape their situations. One of the women in her study explained: "My animals kept me grounded. They were part of my lifeline to say alive. If I wouldn't have had them, I would have been dead . . . ."

As we've seen here, humans' relationship with nonhuman animals is complex. Animals are often among our closest companions, yet subject to terrible abuses. And although there are laws to protect animals from some human abuse, they have no legal rights. Individuals' attitudes about animals (including how you feel about the subjects discussed here) vary widely. Some people have no doubt that animals feel emotions similar to those of humans (love, pain, sadness, happiness, and so on); others are unconvinced. Where you fall on this scale is most certainly related to how you were raised, whether you had animals as pets or farm animals, and what types of relationships you have had with

Who's More Important: The Dog or the Spouse?

When couples split, they have to decide how to divide up property, who has legal custody of the children, and increasingly often, who gets to keep the pets. Sometimes these pet custody battles are even more difficult and expensive than the divorce. Lynn Goldstein, from Jefferson County, Texas, refused to turn over the two cats that a judge had awarded to her ex-husband. She was sentenced to 30 days in jail for defying the court order. In California, Linda Perkins and her ex-husband battled over who would assume custody of their dog—for two years. In the end, Ms. Perkins spent $146,000 in fees. Such cases are becoming increasingly common, prompting some couples to write prenuptials for pets.

animals during your lifetime. Regardless, sociological studies of the human–animal connection reveal much about stratification, oppression, and power in contemporary society and recent sociological attention to animals has broadened our understanding of these issues.

CHILDREN AND SOCIETY

As we saw for animals, society's perceptions and treatment of children are also often inconsistent and contradictory. On the one hand, children in contemporary society are often viewed in very idealistic and sentimental ways. On the other hand, children are often ignored and mistreated.

History and Emergence of Childhood

Because children have not been the focus of much scholarly attention and their writings and art have seldom been preserved, we know very little about children throughout history. One of the most famous books about childhood, *Centuries of Childhood*, was written by Philippe Aries. Aries argued that the concept of childhood did not exist until relatively recently in history. Of course, there were young people in society but Aries argued that these children were not perceived *as children*. Aries studied medieval art to make his case. He notes that paintings during this period rarely depicted children and when they did, artists' drawings of children show them with the bodies and features of adults, just smaller in size. Basically, they were painted, and viewed, as "miniature adults."

Part of the explanation for why children were not seen as separate and distinctly different from adults is that childhood **mortality** rates were high. According to this logic, parents could not invest much in their children because many did not live long. If so many children died young, parents were also not likely to become emotionally attached to them. Linda Pollock, author of *Forgotten Children*, challenged this interpretation. When Pollock examined diaries, autobiographies, and newspaper accounts of legal cases involving child abuse, she found considerable evidence that parents loved and were concerned about their children. She concludes that "nearly all children were wanted, such developmental states as weaning and teething aroused interest and concern, and parents revealed anxiety and distress at the illness or death of their children."

Whether children were viewed as different from adults, and the extent to which they were loved and wanted, remains unclear. But what is clear and interesting about these historical accounts is that children are still viewed through *adults'* lenses. William Corsaro, author of *The Sociology of Childhood,* maintains that society and scholars alike think of children as "adults in process." Seldom do adults appreciate or recognize the richness and creativity of children's cultures and worlds. In other words, adults seldom *really* listen to children but tend to project onto children their own expectations and ideas about who children are (much like what humans do to animals, as we've seen). The focus remains on adult conceptions of children, and children are rarely studied on their own terms. These practices clearly suggest that children are perceived as subordinate and marginal to others, namely adults.

The Innocent Child

Unlike children from earlier centuries, children in contemporary American society are viewed as distinctly different from adults and in need of protection. You are certainly familiar with one of the best examples of this protectionist approach: movie ratings (e.g., PG-13, NC-17). In 1968, the movie rating system was developed to provide parents with information about content of movies so that they could better determine the appropriateness of movies for children, one of many signs that our society views the content of certain movies (and music) as harmful to the innocent minds of young people.

Such protectionist attitudes towards children are also reflected in the legal system. For instance, in 2008 a case was heard before the U.S. Supreme Court to determine whether child rapists should receive the death penalty, a punishment historically used only in cases involving murder. The Supreme Court decided that the death penalty was not a "proportional punishment for the rape of a child" and therefore could not be applied unless a life was taken. Many legislators were appalled and vowed to fight the decision. What made this case even more interesting is that victim advocacy groups representing rape victims and rape crisis centers supported the Court's decision. A spokesperson noted that children are typically abused by a family member or close family friend and applying the death penalty to these individuals would mean that the child, who has already undergone tremendous trauma, is likely to feel further burdened knowing she or he played a role in sending a family member or friend to death row. Although people spoke out on both sides of this issue, they all shared the same assumption—that a child is vulnerable, powerless, and in need of special protection.

No one denies that crimes against children are horrific, that perpetrators deserve punishment, or that certain media is too graphic and "adult" for children's good. But sociologists are not so much interested in whether children in fact are in need of protection or not. What interests sociologists is the fact that society has *defined* children as individuals in need of such protection and reasons why this has occurred. It is important to remember here that children haven't always been viewed as so helpless and vulnerable. Major cultural shifts in attitudes towards certain groups do not just *happen*, they are spurred by larger cultural, social, political, and historical shifts. So what might have brought about these new perceptions?

One explanation for why children came to be viewed as persons in need of special care focuses on the role of economic forces in transforming parent–child relationships. Prior to the 19th century, most children were seen as workers and worked alongside their parents to produce whatever resources were needed, including food, clothing, shelter, and so on. After the Industrial Revolution, society shifted to a **consumption model**—family members went to factories to work and purchased the resources they needed with their wages. Initially, children worked in factories along with their parents. This began to change, however, when efforts to regulate child labor intensified in the 19th and 20th centuries. Reformers believed children should not be subject to the dangerous conditions in factories. Of course, when children left the factories, someone needed to look out for them and so it was that during this period, women's roles became primarily associated with the home and childrearing.

Today, children continue to be viewed as innocent, precious, and in need of protection. It is significant that many people also believe that *mothers* are the best persons to fill this role and if possible, they should stay home to care for their children. Perhaps not coincidentally, these cultural debates over whether women should stay home with the kids or work outside the home intensified precisely during the period when women were gaining greater power and status in society, and men's status as economic providers was eroding. This is also the period when there was much media attention and public panic about "missing children," razor blades in Halloween candy, school shootings, and so on, creating fear among parents that their children might be taken from them any minute and that strangers pose serious danger. In reality, there is little or no evidence that children are in such danger. For instance, sociologist Joel Best investigated the cases where strangers allegedly poisoned children's Halloween candy and found there was no basis for these claims. Such tales, however, serve to create anxiety among parents that their children can be victimized by strangers at any time, and the idea that they require constant supervision (preferably from the mother). These beliefs reinforce the existing stratification system by making it harder for women to gain more financial independence and power in society.

Child Poverty

It is ironic that children in the United States are perceived as precious, vulnerable, and in need of protection because children are especially vulnerable to poverty in this country. According to the National Center for Children in Poverty (NCCP), 19 percent (14 million) of American children live in poverty. This means that their families earn less than what the federal government deems to be the poverty line, which is a mere $22,050 for a family of four. The situation for children is getting worse: Between 2005 and 2008, there was a 21 percent increase in the number of children living in poverty.

There are several factors associated with child poverty, including the race, ethnicity, and age of the child, and immigrant status of parents. White children are least likely to live in poverty (about 11 percent), and black children are most likely to be poor (about 35 percent). Nearly 1 in 4 children of immigrant parents are officially poor, compared to 17 percent of children in nonimmigrant

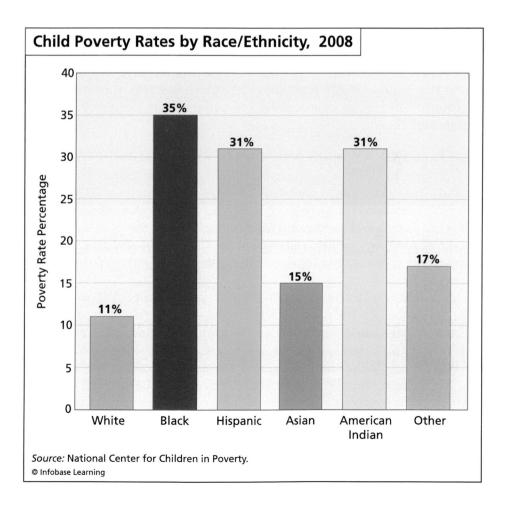

Child Poverty Rates by Race/Ethnicity, 2008

Source: National Center for Children in Poverty.
© Infobase Learning

families. Finally, young children are especially vulnerable to living in poverty. About 22 percent of children younger than age 6 live in poor families.

Children who live in poverty face serious hardships. They are likely to experience food insecurity and lack health insurance; they are also more likely to suffer poor cognitive development and learning disabilities. Poverty contributes to behavioral, emotional, and social problems among children. According to the NCCP, children who experience poverty (especially African American children) are more likely to be poor as adults.

Child Abuse and Neglect

It might surprise you to learn that there were laws preventing the cruelty of animals long before there were laws governing the maltreatment of children. In the United States, the American Society for the Prevention of Cruelty to Animals (ASPCA) was founded in 1886; it wasn't until 1974 that Congress passed the Child Abuse Prevention and Treatment Act.

Children are one of the most vulnerable groups in society, partly because they are subject to significant levels of abuse from those who are responsible for their care—parents. In fact, about 3.5 million children were investigated by Child Protective Services in 2007. Many of these children were very young—32 percent were younger than 4 years. According to the U.S. Department of Health and Human Services, an estimated 794,000 children were victims of maltreatment in 2007 alone.

THE STATUS OF ANIMALS AND CHILDREN WORLDWIDE

The treatment of children and animals in many parts of the world is deeply troubling. Positioned on the lowest social status rungs, both are often subject to extreme neglect and exploitation. It is difficult to draw conclusions about the status of animals worldwide because laws concerning animal abuse and cruelty vary significantly by country, and enforcement also varies widely. But several organizations have led efforts to track child abuse and exploitation throughout the world.

The World Health Organization (WHO) reports that 40 million children under the age of 15 are abused and neglected around the world. According to the International Labor Organization, 246 million children (ages 5–17) currently labor under conditions that are illegal, extremely exploitative, or hazardous. Worldwide, children are vulnerable to **human trafficking**; they are taken from their homes, often by force but sometimes sold by parents, and forced to provide labor or services, such as domestic work. In some cases, babies or young children are sold to couples wanting to adopt children. In fact, according to a recent UNICEF report, between 1,000 and 1,500 babies and children from Guatemala are sold each year for adoption to couples in North America and Europe.

Another type of trafficking that has received attention in recent years is sex trafficking, also known as **sex slavery**. Young girls or boys may be lured from

Helping Children and Animals

Although children and animals are limited in their ability to speak for themselves, there are powerful advocates for both groups. In some cases, these are individuals who make simple (but perhaps difficult) choices every day to help a child in need or prevent an animal from being killed or harmed. For example, thousands of adults report suspected cases of child abuse, even when doing so might endanger their own safety or lifestyle. Others volunteer to serve as Court Appointed Special Advocates (CASA) or tutor underprivileged youth. Some individuals are involved in animal rescue organizations, often volunteering time at animal shelters or fostering animals in their own homes. **Vegetarians** (people who eat no meat, including fish, beef, or poultry) and **vegans** (vegetarians who also do not eat eggs or any dairy products) often report that they gave up eating meat in order to avoid contributing to abuse and deaths of animals. There are also hundreds of organizations and social movements working to protect children and animals. If you are interested in finding ways to better the lives of children or animals, check out what is happening in your own community.

their homes (sometimes with the promise of making a lot of money to help support their families) and forced into prostitution. It is estimated that about one-third of all sex workers (or prostitutes) in the Mekong sub-region of Southeast Asia are between 12 and 17 years old. Another form of violence against girls that has received attention in recent years is **female genital cutting** (FGC). This practice involves cutting and removing parts of the girls' genitalia, usually under unsterile conditions and with no anesthesia. According to the WHO, it is estimated that more than 100 million girls and women alive today have experienced FGC; in Africa alone, about 3 million girls are at risk for FGC each year.

SUMMARY

Arguably, children and animals occupy the lowest rungs of the stratification ladder. Of the two, animals certainly fall at the bottom. For the most part, the lives of *all* humans—even those who are held in low regard such as prisoners or terrorists—are more highly valued than the lives of *all* nonhuman animals. Millions of animals are euthanized yearly, whereas the death penalty for humans is used sparingly. If we assume abuse is likely to be inflicted on those who are perceived to be less powerful, the fact that animals are sometimes subject to abuse by children suggests that on some level children perceive themselves to be superior to animals. But as we've seen in this chapter, both children's and animals' positions in society are defined by their nearly complete dependence upon those in power, and both groups are particularly vulnerable to maltreatment by those in power.

Further Reading

Ascione, Frank R., and Phil Arkow. *Child Abuse, Domestic Violence, and Animal Abuse: Linking the Circles of Compassion for Prevention and Intervention*. West Lafayette, Ind: Purdue University Press, 1999.

Atwood-Harvey, Dana. "From touchstone to tombstone: Children's experiences with the abuse of their beloved pets." *Humanity & Society* 31 (2007): 379-400.

Child Labor Public Education Project: Causes of Child Labor. Available online at http://www.continuetolearn.uiowa.edu/laborctr/child_labor/about/causes.html. Accessed February 3, 2010.

Corsaro, William. *The Sociology of Childhood*. Thousand Oaks, Calif.: Pine Forge Press, 1997.

Fitzgerald, Amy J. "'They gave me a reason to live': The protective effects of companion animals on the suicidality of abused women." *Humanity & Society* 31 (2007): 355-378.

Melson, Gail F. *Why the Wild Things Are: Animals in the Lives of Children*. Cambridge, Mass.: Harvard University Press, 2001.

Morell, Virginia. Minds of their own. *National Geographic,* March 2008. Available at http://ngm.nationalgeographic.com/2008/03/animal-minds/virginia-morell-text. Accessed February 1, 2010.

Pollock, Linda A. *Forgotten Children: Parent-Child Relations from 1500 to 1900*. Cambridge: Cambridge University Press, 1987.

UNICEF: Child protection from violence, exploitation and abuse. Available online at http://www.unicef.org/protection/index_exploitation.html. Accessed January 25, 2010.

CHAPTER 6

GLOBAL INEQUALITIES

Social stratification exists not only *within* particular societies but also *among* societies—that is, on an international or global level. As we have discussed in previous chapters, stratification creates inequalities among groups of people, which results in people having different access to resources, power, and prestige. The same thing exists among nations and groups of people around the globe. A young boy in the United States, for example, may take for granted a quality education, as well as the amenities that accompany it—healthy school lunches and sports programs. A young boy in Mali, however, may not be able to attend primary or secondary school, unless his parents can pay school fees. If they cannot afford these fees, he may never learn to read. His sports agenda may be confined to kicking a homemade soccer ball down a dusty street.

Such global inequalities are becoming more pronounced—and certainly more visible—as we move into the 21st century because the planet is undergoing rapid **globalization**, a process through which the lives of human beings living in very different parts of the world are becoming more and more interconnected. Because of globalization, we are becoming dependent on one another in almost every social sphere—economically, culturally, politically. We eat fresh blueberries in the winter because they are flown to our local markets from Chile. We chat with our friends living or traveling in distant countries via Facebook or video-conference with them for free on Skype. We participate vicariously in the political decisions of other nations, watching events such as the revolution in Egypt "live" via satellite and cable television.

But not all aspects of our global connectedness are positive. The cell phones we use every day, for example, would not work without small parts that are created in **sweatshop factories** (workplaces that subject workers to extreme economic exploitation and often physical abuse) in Asia. In fact, our cell phone technology would not even be *possible* without a substance called *coltan*, which is mined in the Congo by young men who live on less than $2 per day. In other words, the interdependence of human beings around the world is evident in everything around us—our food, our technology, our recreation. But, as the examples above illustrate, this interdependence is not always fair or equal because not everyone benefits from globalization or experiences it in the same way.

THE ROOTS OF GLOBALIZATION

Globalization has its roots in the **colonization** of the Third World (or the Global South) by Western industrialized nations. Historically, colonization served to establish markets for colonizing countries in far-flung areas of the globe while, at the same time, enabling the colonizers to extract goods (rubber, copper, gold) or services (cheap labor) from the colonized country. Chief among the colonizing countries of the 18th and 19th centuries were Belgium, France, Great Britain, the Netherlands, and Spain. Belgium's conquest and exploitation of the Congo, for example, is one of the prime examples of the grim exploitation

King Baudouin, from Belgium, visits a military school in the Belgian Congo in 1955. *(Wikipedia. CongoPresse)*

of a developing country's natural and human resources by a developed nation. Recent best sellers, including the novel *Poisonwood Bible* by Barbara Kingsolver and nonfiction account *In the Footsteps of Mr. Kurtz*, vividly illustrate how colonization of the Congo bred economic exploitation, human degradation, and the violation of basic human rights that have persisted to this day.

Although we think of colonization as something that happened a long time ago, it is actually still going on today. Wealthy countries, like the United States and its allies, are still able to use their muscle to push around smaller, less developed nations. In other words, we still see powerful countries exerting economic leverage over smaller, poorer nations to gain access to resources and labor in those countries. But now the "colonizing" is done not only through armies and territorial invasions (those still happen) but through international economic institutions, treaties, and policies.

HOW GLOBAL INEQUALITIES ARE MAINTAINED

Globalization and global stratification are maintained through social institutions, like banks and schools. Most of these institutions now have a global focus

Talking About Our World

First World	A term originating during the Cold War era to describe developed nations, particularly those allied with the United States. Today this term is seen as politically incorrect because it implies that developed nations are more important or "better" than developing or nondeveloped nations.
Third World	During the Cold War, the term referred to nonaligned nations—that is, those siding neither with the United State (first world) nor with the Soviet Union (second world). After the Cold War, the term came to refer to developing or nondeveloped nations, with high rates of poverty and illiteracy (e.g., Indonesia, Jamaica). Although still used today, the term is being replaced by the term "Two-Thirds World" (see below).
Global North	Countries, mostly in the Northern hemisphere, with a high human development index. According to the United Nations, the human development index is above .8 (1 is highest possible score). *
Global South	Countries, mostly in the Southern hemisphere, with a medium (less than .8) or low human (less than .5) human development index.*
Two-Thirds World	Another name for the Third World, which seeks to show that the Two-Thirds world is large and diverse, in scope, demographics, cultures, and politics. It implies that the First World is, in fact, the smaller portion of the globe and the Two-Thirds World represents the majority of people on the planet.

Source: United Nations Human Development Reports (HDR), 2005

and, almost without our realizing it, they socialize us into a globalized world. For example, we take it for granted that we can put our ATM card into a bank machine in Tanzania or Zanzibar and receive cash in a few seconds. The banks' computers talk to each other much faster and easier than we do and with no need for an interpreter. You may remember a recent television commercial about a Western couple stranded in what appeared to be a North African or middle-Eastern location. They were "rescued" by a little boy who beckoned them to follow him. In halting English he said, "Atiem can help you." Thinking Atiem was a person, the couple followed the child, only to find he was leading them to an ATM machine, from which they procured cash for their emergency.

ATM machines are found in most urban and rural locations around the world, symbolizing the wide-reaching arm of economic globalization. *(Wikipedia)*

In the world of economic globalization, they needed little human help, only the help of a mechanized agent of the transnational economy.

Economic Institutions

Behind the ATM machine in the desert is a world of powerful global economic institutions and multinational corporations. **Multinational corporations** are corporations that engage in production, manufacturing, and marketing components in *multiple* countries. Within this construct, various (often poorer) nations are the source of production for a particular product, which is marketed in other (often richer) nations. Moving capital freely across borders enables these corporations to take advantage of cheap labor in one part of the world, while maximizing the sale of products in a wealthier segment of the globe.

Educational Institutions

Our educational institutions have also "gone global," with a rapid increase in the number of students from developing nations attending colleges and universities in the United States and other Western nations. Such intermingling of cultures and opinions adds diversity to our campuses and encourages cross-cultural learning experiences. However, another side to the globalization of education is not so positive. For example, Americans have become increasingly insecure about their students' ability to compete in a global forum for top university placements and for good jobs after graduation. Consequently, many concerned high school and university boards and administrators have begun promoting science and technology over other, "softer" subjects, in an effort to ensure that their graduates can compete in a global marketplace with students from China, Japan, and India. The institutional concern over students' ability to compete on a global basis has generated concern among parents and teachers, who worry about young students suffering stress from standardized testing, pressure to produce good grades, and from the increasing demands of longer school days and fewer (or shorter) vacations. It also means that many young people are no longer exposed to the arts, culture, and physical education, as these courses are the first to go when schools increase curricular requirements in science and technology.

Cultural Ideology

In order for one group (e.g., nation) to exploit another for labor or natural resources, the exploitive group must feel a sense of entitlement. That is, there must be a belief that it is completely acceptable, even morally correct, that another country's land or resources (including human resources) should be used for another's benefit. In the United States, we have a strong sense of privacy and ownership, and we would be appalled if someone else simply took over what we believed was our own. Imagine your next door neighbor cutting down trees in your backyard to use for his firewood—without asking or perhaps offering you $200 for the whole lot. If you're poor and desperate to pay your bills this month, you might accept this pitiful offer, even though it means that you won't have any wood to warm your own house next winter. In essence, this is a process that occurs worldwide. Richer, more powerful countries exploit poorer and less powerful countries that lack the political or economic resources to fight back or to refuse offers that will eventually lead to their own downfall.

For Western cultures, this sense of entitlement stems from **capitalism**, which is the economic system in which the "means of production" (the "stuff" from which materials are produced) are owned by a few individuals. Those that actually produce the goods—the workers—work for those who own the means of production and receive compensation for their labor. But wealth is held in the hands of the owners, not the workers, who are often poor and whose quality of life is affected by the imbalance of power and wealth. Part of what drives capitalism is the belief that those with the best ideas and greatest means can acquire massive wealth, and that this wealth need not be redistributed to workers or others who have neither the ideas nor the means (or may have the ideas but lack the means) to promote them. This system often involves paying workers very little so profits can be maximized. Indeed, the primary goal of capitalism is to continually increase profit.

You can probably see how such a system promotes the idea that capitalists are *entitled* to whatever wealth and fortune they can legally acquire. If you've grown up in the United States (or in some other capitalist society), chances are you see nothing wrong with this system, as long as what occurs within the system is done legally. But herein lies a problem. The United States was founded on the underlying value of human dignity, a value that was emphasized when Thomas Jefferson wrote in the U.S. Declaration of Independence, "We hold these truths to be self-evident, that all men are created equal, that they are endowed by their Creator with certain unalienable Rights, that among these are Life, Liberty, and the Pursuit of Happiness."

Indeed, most Americans believe that workers should be paid a fair wage and very few would support the exploitation of workers. And, these same values are reflected in U.S. laws that prohibit unfair labor practices, including sweatshops. At the same time, most Americans also know that many workers overseas are exploited, especially those who work for a pittance to produce goods that are sold cheaply in the United States. The question that arises here is how can people reconcile exploitation of workers (or whole nations of people) with a belief in the rightness and legitimacy of an economic system that, by design, legitimates maximizing profit for a few by using whatever resources (human or otherwise) available? How is this contradiction in values possible to maintain?

Made in China

In 2010, some companies in China increased their hourly payments to workers. Among these was Foxconn Technology (the company that manufactures the Apple iPhone and Dell computer parts), which doubled workers' salaries to about $300 per month.

What led them to increase workers' wages? Did Foxconn Technology suddenly and generously decide to share its enormous profits with those who produce their products? Probably not. The decision was more than likely the result of several tragic and very public suicides of Foxconn Technology workers. The first Foxconn worker to commit suicide was 19 year old Ma Xiangqian. According to *The New York Times*, "Mr. Ma's pay stub shows that he worked 286 hours in the month before he died, including 112 hours of overtime, about three times the legal limit. For all of that, even with extra pay for overtime, he earned the equivalent of $1 an hour." (http://www.nytimes.com/2010/06/07/business/global/07suicide.html)

Electronics factory in Shenzhen, China, where workers likely work long hours for little pay. *(Wikipedia. Photo by Steve Jurvetson)*

Some individuals are aware of, but disregard, the poor working conditions and low pay of workers in other countries because they are ignorant of the conditions facing these people and the nations in which they live. We often hear from our students, for example, that it's okay to pay a Chinese worker 75 cents per hour because it's so cheap to live in China. But this opinion fails to acknowledge that workers in China are not happy with that 75 cents per hour, and that workers' protests about low wages have forced manufacturing companies in China to increase wages (see sidebar).

Another important cultural ideology that allows such a system to go unquestioned by many is "othering." As we discussed in Chapter 1, othering occurs when those individuals in power are perceived as the "normal" and desirable group, and individuals who do not fall within that group are perceived as different, "less than," and inferior. The belief that one's own group (in this case, country) or practice (in this case, capitalism) is superior to other countries or systems, can lead to a sense of superiority over others. From there, it is fairly easy to see others as lacking the same rights and privileges of ourselves. There are plenty of obvious examples of othering that have occurred throughout history, including the atrocious treatment of Jews during the Holocaust or the kidnapping of Africans for the slave trade. Such atrocities can occur only if those who perpetrate them see others as inferior—less than human. On some level, such attitudes persist. Today they are (consciously or unconsciously) directed at people in developing countries so that exploitation of their lands, resources, and service can continue.

In short, social institutions today are organized on a global level. They function on the macro level, a level of activity that overarches the micro (individual) level. Sometimes, these globalized institutions benefit us—if we need that ATM machine in the desert, for example, it will be there. At other times, they create and maintain gross inequalities among people around the planet, often with tragic consequences (like the impoverishment and exploitation of millions). Ideologies serve to keep these systems in place by justifying the systems that give rise to global stratification and inequality.

CONSEQUENCES OF GLOBALIZATION FOR WORKERS

One result of economic globalization is that corporations are now able to move materials and goods (capital) easily within and between countries. Consequently, a company may decide to produce goods and services in the lowest cost location and take advantage of cheap labor in China or India, for example. In such countries workers are often paid very low wages and are subjected to extremely poor worker-safety standards. Workers may have few rights; they are seldom in a position to organize unions or advocate for better pay. Pollution standards may also be low in these locations, allowing corporations to skirt environmental standards that would be taken-for-granted in Western nations.

Slums near a garbage dump in Indonesia. Multinational corporations often pollute as they manufacture in developing countries. Ironically, the products they manufacture for export often return to the developing world as waste. *(Wikipedia. Photo by Jonathan McIntosh)*

Young workers perform final testing on electronic drives in China. *(Wikipedia. Photo by Robert Scoble)*

International factories and assembly plants of this kind have become known as sweatshops.

Sweatshops are primarily workplaces in the developing world, but also exist (usually illegally) in the United States and in other industrialized nations. Working conditions in sweatshops are extraordinarily difficult and hazardous for employees. China (as the sidebar presented earlier in this chapter suggests) has become notorious for its sweatshop labor and the brutal conditions of its factories. In the book *Factory Girls*, reporter Leslie Chang describes the harsh factory conditions that many young girls experience as they work on the assembly lines in the industrial city of Dongguan. Chang describes the mass migration of girls and young women from rural poverty to urban factories, where they are put to work in manufacturing plants that produce jeans, sneakers, computers, or Christmas tree ornaments. She estimates that approximately 130 million workers have moved from rural China to urbanized areas to work in factories owned by multinational corporations, making this **collective dislocation** the largest migration in human history.

When corporations move jobs to countries with cheap labor, that movement also has an effect on nations in the developed world. Workers in countries such as the United States and other industrialized nations may find themselves losing their jobs to workers in developing nations. After the passage of the **North American Free Trade Agreement (NAFTA)**, for example, many companies moved manufacturing jobs across the border into Mexico, where they could take advantage of cheaper labor and less stringent worker safety and environmental laws. The American company Maytag serves as a prime example of an iconic American company that has closed plants in the United States and shifted production to developing nations. It may seem ironic that Maytag moved jobs out of the United States and into Third World nations because many of us have grown up with the image of a Maytag washing machine as an "all-American" product. Nevertheless, in 1996, Maytag's decision to utilize Mexican labor devastated American towns like Galesburg, Illinois, where Maytag had been the town's largest employer for decades. According to David Moberg, a writer for *In These Times*, when Maytag closed its Galesburg plant, it sent about 1,600 American jobs to a new Maytag plant in Reynosa, Mexico. Maytag also sent work to Daewoo, a Korean subcontractor, which proposed building its own plant in Mexico. Although the local Machinists' union in Galesburg opposed the plant shutdown, the American workers could not prevail against strong laws and treaties (such as NAFTA) that now protect multinational corporations. Since 2000, according to Moberg, approximately 2.7 million manufacturing jobs have been lost in the United States as companies like Maytag moved their production base out of the country.

Workers in industrialized nations may also be affected by **outsourcing**, which is the practice of contracting to workers in developing countries much of the service work that was once performed in the United States. You probably experience the effects of outsourcing yourself more often than you might think. When you report a software problem on your computer, you may find yourself speaking to a service representative in India. When you wire money via Western Union, you may do so via an employee in Russia or Mexico. Whether we consumers have our questions answered and our problems solved when we talk to agents in India or Russia is a subject for another venue and another

Floor of a Maytag factory in the early 20th century. Maytag closed several U.S. plants when it moved its operations to Mexico. *(Library of Congress)*

debate. What is *not* debatable, however, is that the jobs being performed by these international representatives of multinational corporations were once jobs that resided here at home. Perhaps your father, aunt, or cousin has been laid off because his or her job was outsourced to an employee in India who was willing to accept a lower wage or work longer hours for doing the same work.

Consequences of Globalization for Women

Sociologists Stanley Eitzen and Maxine Baca Zinn have pointed out that women's paid and unpaid work is one of the cornerstones of globalization. Indeed, women have been called the invisible foot soldiers of globalization, ranging from the young girls in Chinese factories described above to women closer to home—those from Mexico and Central America who work in maquiladora factories near the U.S.-Mexico border.

Maquiladoras, a direct off-shoot of globalization, are factories along the U.S.-Mexico border where workers assemble products for export. There are more than 3,000 maquiladora factories on the Mexican side of the border, and these plants employ about 1.3 million Mexicans, many of them women. But

Women work in a maquiladora factory near the border between the United States and Mexico. *(Wikipedia)*

the products the workers assemble do not originate in Mexico. Instead, they are composed of pieces that are often exported with little or no tariff *from* the United States to be assembled by cheap labor in Mexico and then shipped *back* to the country of origin or to other industrialized nations. Trade agreements like NAFTA minimize or eliminate cross-border tariffs, making the export/import process uncomplicated and cost-effective for multinational corporations.

Maquiladora factories have become notorious for their exploitation of female employees, who work at about one-sixth of the American hourly wage. Women workers in maquiladoras report long hours without bathroom breaks; harsh working conditions, such as standing or sitting in one position for many hours; sexual harassment and rape by employers; and employers who refuse to allow them to organize for better working conditions.

Ongoing sexual predation exists in and around maquiladora factories. Because many women leave their homes in interior parts of Mexico to work in border factories, they often live alone or with other women near the factory or plant. They may also be forced to work nights and, therefore, must walk or travel back and forth to work in darkness. According to Diana Washington Valdez, hundreds of women have been murdered in the border city of Ciudad Juarez since 1993, many of them maquiladora employees. Autopsies have revealed many of them were raped and tortured before being killed. Police seem unable or unwilling to ascertain the cause of the femicides. But local residents blame the maquiladoras, partly because factory bosses are reported to have connections to local drug cartels and, more generally, because maquiladoras have created a population of displaced, vulnerable women—far from home and at the mercy of factory owners.

Women are also negatively affected by the globalization of the electronics industry. Anibel Ferus-Comelo reports that many production workers in the international electronics industry are young women. Furthermore, these young women are often migrants—that is, they have moved from their home or origin (often from another country) for the specific purpose of working in an electronics plant. According to Ferus-Comelo, between 1985 and 2000, women represented more than half of the electronics labor force in such places as Hong Kong, Singapore, Taiwan, Malaysia, Thailand, Sri Lanka, the Czech Republic, and Puerto Rico. She points out that this **feminization of migration** is continuing, as women migrate from countries like Bangladesh to the cities such as Hong Kong and Singapore, where high-tech factories are booming. Women factory workers earn less than their male counterparts. They may also be forced to work compulsory overtime for no extra pay. Furthermore, many migrant women live in hostels or dormitories run by or associated with the factory. This enables bosses and managers to monitor women's lives even when they are not at work.

Globalization has also given rise to another kind of female migration—the movement of female caretakers or nannies, who are migrating from the developing world to the developed world to care for children of First World families. Barbara Ehrenreich and Arlie Russell Hochschild have called this migration of women the "underside of globalization." As First World women have increasingly joined the workforce in developed nations like the United States, a **care deficit** has been created. That is, First World women, who have increasingly taken jobs outside their homes, need other women to replace them or assist them with childcare, elder care, and housework. Thus, millions of women from poor countries in the Global South are moving to developed nations to perform traditional "women's work" that more affluent women no longer have time to do. Most migrating women take up work as domestics or maids, often sending their meager wages to families in their country of origin.

Ehrenreich and Hochschild point out, however, that this ongoing stream of domestic workers into the United States and other industrialized nations has little to do with American women's reluctance to do house and/or care work. Instead, it is a symptom of our downsized economy, which has forced many American women to seek employment outside the home because families often

Women (often women of color) from developing nations migrate to industrialized nations for jobs as domestics and nannies. *(Shutterstock)*

cannot survive on a single salary. At the same time, unlike women in many other post-industrial countries, women in the United States do not have social services that fund child care (in the home or outside the home). Many of the after-school programs that once provided care for children of working mothers have been cut or have lost their funding, making it impossible for American women to juggle in-home and out-of-home tasks. A mother who used to pick her children up at 6 p.m., after a school-based sports program, now must find a way to leave her job at 3 p.m. because the after-school program has been scrapped. Consequently, the *increasing* number of women in the workforce and the *decreasing* number of social services for children and families creates a deficit that is filled by nannies and domestics from Mexico, Cuba, Haiti, and other developing nations.

This globalization of women's care work provides much-needed support for women in countries like the United States. However, it is important to view the flip-side of this arrangement and to ask what effects it has on the families of the immigrant women. As Ehrenreich and Hochschild point out, migrating women often leave their own young children behind to be cared for by mothers, grandmothers, sisters, or even older daughters. This creates familial disruption, stress, and loneliness on both sides of the border. Rhacel Parrenas, who studied Filipino migrant mothers, points out the high cost of globalization on such transnational families. Because it is very difficult for families to retain strong ties over great distances, many women lose touch with their children, siblings, and spouses for months or years at a time. Women interviewed by Perrenas report that the loss of time spent together cannot be replaced. In fact, filling the care deficit in First World countries creates a reciprocal deficit of care in the Global south. Thus, the globalization of women's work creates a huge divide between women in the wealthiest countries and those in the poorest ones.

Online Resources on Globalization

Organization	Mission	Web Address
Equal Exchange	Promotes fair trade among farmers in the developing world	www.equalexchange.com
Food First	Combats poverty and hunger	www.foodfirst.org
Global Exchange	Builds people-to-people ties through reality tours, fair trade, and human rights campaigns	www.globalexchange.org
World Social Forum	Organizes open meetings where individuals and groups opposed to global inequality share ideas and strategies	www.formumsocialmundial.org.br
Women for Women International	Helps women survivors of war rebuild their lives	www.womenforwomen.org

Source: Modified from Eitzen and Baca Zinn (2009)

Although they may be living or working in the same town and the same home, they are separated by what Ehrenreich and Hochschild call a great divide of privilege and opportunity.

Perhaps one positive aspect of this privilege gap is that it is visible to those of us living here in the developed world. When Third World women appear at our schools and playgrounds, we are forced to confront the realities of globalization as they appear in our own towns and communities. Indeed, when people in the developed world are educated about global inequalities, we often respond by wanting to promote social change. Although we are at the top of the ladder of privilege, there is still much that we can do to mitigate the inequalities of our rapidly globalizing planet.

SUMMARY

Stratification among different societies around the globe is increasing. The gap between the very rich and the extremely poor is widening every day. Yet, at the same time, there are aspects of globalization that have the *potential* to bring people together in new and unique ways that might mitigate the social inequality globalization breeds. After all, we now meet each other on the Internet and enjoy video calls on our cell phones. Social networks connect students in Manhattan and Tokyo with rural villages in Africa and Nepal. In fact, social networking sites have become a new venue for organizing for social change. The recent revolt in Egypt, which toppled a leader who had held power for 30 years, is being called a Facebook revolution.

Further Reading

Brecher, Jeremy, Tim Costello, and Brendan Smith. *Globalization from Below.* Boston: South End Press, 2000.

Chang, Leslie T. *Factory Girls: From Village to City in a Changing China.* New York: Spiegel and Grau, 2009.

Ehrenreich, Barbara, and Arlie Russell Hochschild. *Global Woman: Nannies, Maids, and Sex Workers in the New Economy.* New York: Henry Holt and Company, 2002.

Eitzen, D. Stanley, and Maxine Baca Zinn. *Globalization: The Transformation of Social Worlds.* Belmont, Calif.: Wadsworth, 2009.

Ferus-Comelo, Anibel. Double jeopardy: Gender and migration in electronics manufacturing. In *Challenging the Chip,* edited by Ted Smith, David A. Sonnenfield, and David Naguib, 42–54. Philadelphia: Temple University Press, 2006.

Kingsolver, Barbara. *The Poisonwood Bible.* New York: Harper Flamingo, 1990.

Parrenas, Rhacel Salazar. The care crisis in the Philippines: Children and transnational families in the new global economy. In *Global Woman: Nannies, Maids, and Sex Workers in the New Economy,* edited by Barbara Ehrenreich and Arlie Russell Hochschild, 39–54. New York: Henry Holt and Company, 2003.

Prieto, Norma Iglesias. *Beautiful Flowers of the Maquiladora: Life Histories of Women Workers in Tijuana.* Austin: University of Texas Press, 1997.

Shiva, Vandana. *Staying Alive: Women, Ecology, and Development.* Boston: South End Press, 2010.

Valdez, Diana Washington. *The Killing Fields: Harvest of Women.* Austin: Peace at the Border Press, 2006.

Wrong, Michela. *In the Footsteps of Mr. Kurtz: Living on the Brink of Disaster in Mobutu's Congo.* New York: Harper, 2002.

CHAPTER 7

REDUCING INEQUALITIES

INTRODUCTION

The consequences of social inequality are very real and affect society on every level of social interaction: individual, group, institutional. Those who are not oppressed enjoy invisible advantage in the form of privilege: class privilege, white privilege, male privilege, straight privilege—all very powerful forces that serve to benefit certain groups at the expense of others. On average, privileged people have better access to scarce resources, live longer, hold greater wealth and power, and enjoy myriad other social benefits. We are not stating that people belonging to privileged groups *intend* to infringe on the rights of others. But the effect is the same.

Because we all hold a stake in the outcomes of other groups as well as our own, we must recognize privilege, understand how it works, and further, learn how it can be used to advance social justice for everyone. One thing that complicates the fight for equality is the fact that most Americans continue to look up (at where they aspire to be) rather than down (where those less fortunate are and where no one aspires to be). This perspective often means turning a blind eye to issues facing others (and sometimes themselves). Most of us are raised to believe that everyone has equal access to power and resources in society. As we've pointed out in this volume, however, there are *structural* inequalities that affect millions of Americans and many millions more worldwide. Fortunately, there are many individuals and organizations working hard to "level the playing field." This final chapter provides a glimpse into some of the past and present efforts to protect certain groups who continue to face considerable inequality in society. We begin where we left off in the last chapter—fighting global inequality—then explore efforts to reduce inequalities and oppression in the United States.

FIGHTING GLOBAL INEQUALITY
Outcry Against Sweatshops
One of the first issues around which people in the industrialized world mobilized was the exposure of child labor and the rampant abuse of women in sweatshops by well-known American companies, such as Gap, NIKE, and Wal-Mart. Public consciousness about sweatshops emerged in the 1990s when the National Labor Committee incited a huge public outcry by exposing the use of child labor in the creation of Kathie Lee Gifford's clothing label, which was being distributed through Wal-Mart. Gifford later disavowed sweatshops but not before a huge segment of the American public decried such labor practices by boycotting her clothing line and the stores where it was sold. Shortly after the Gifford expose, an organization called Students United Against Sweatshops became

A strong and growing anti-sweatshop movement has taken root in many industrialized nations. A police officer speaks with a UNITE HERE protestor. *(Wikipedia. Photo by Ben Schumin)*

active on college campuses across the United States and Canada, urging other students to look at the labels on their clothes and to follow the trail of sweatshop labor that went into the production of their t-shirts, blue jeans, and sneakers.

The Anti-Globalization Movement

A somewhat different and more overarching movement against globalization also arose in the 1990s. That movement, simply known as the **Anti-Globalization Movement,** gained momentum when the **General Agreement on Tariffs and Trades (GATT)**, which had existed since the 1940s, was replaced by the **World Trade Organization (WTO)** in 1995. The purpose of the WTO was (and is) to promote the interests of free trade and streamline multinational activities. For example, among the WTO's top agenda items are the promotion of free trade; the creation of free trade zones with small or no tariffs; the reduction or elimination of capital controls over multinational corporations; and the harmonization of intellectual property laws across the majority of states. Protests, particularly by students and young people in general, sprang up around the developed world, leading to large-scale, sometimes violent public demonstrations against globalization. Protesters cited concern for quality of life among workers, both in developed and developing nations, but were particularly vocal about child labor, forced labor, environmental destruction, and violations of national sovereignty in the **Global South** (a term used to refer to those parts of the world that have greatly suffered from the effects of globalization). Large and vociferous protests were held in Seattle in 1999; in Washington, D.C., in 2000; and in Genoa, Italy, in 2001. As frustration and emotions boiled on both sides, these demonstrations degenerated into riots from which the host cities took months, if not years, to recover.

With the passage of GATT and the establishment of the WTO, an anti-globalization movement has arisen in industrialized nations. *(Wikipedia)*

Labor unions, such as the AFL-CIO and UNITE HERE have also condemned sweatshops, encouraging American workers to see the connection between the loss of jobs in U.S. companies and the transfer of those jobs to egregiously exploited workers in poverty-stricken nations. Nonetheless, the drain

Movies That Inspire

Over the years, many films and television movies have highlighted amazing life stories that both inspire and unite people around the United States, or even around the world. Some of these films are based on true stories, while others are dramatizations of actual events, or even purely fictional accounts intended to demonstrate the struggle for equality. The following is an eclectic list of just a few of these inspirational films*:

City of God (2003)
Two boys growing up in a violent neighborhood of Rio de Janeiro take different paths: one becomes a photographer, the other a drug dealer.

Daughters of the Dust (1992)
Languid look at the Gullah culture of the Sea Islands off the coast of South Carolina and Georgia where African folk-ways were maintained well into the 20th Century and was one of the last bastions of these mores in America. Set in 1902.

Gandhi (1982)
Biography of 'Mahatma Gandhi', the lawyer who became the famed leader of the Indian revolts against the British through his philosophy of non-violent protest.

Iron-Jawed Angels (2004)
Defiant young activists take the women's suffrage movement by storm, putting their lives at risk to help American women win the right to vote.

Made in Dagenham (2010)
A dramatization of the 1968 strike at the Ford Dagenham car plant, where female workers walked out in protest against sexual discrimination.

Matewan (1987)
A labor union organizer comes to an embattled mining community brutally and violently dominated and harassed by the mining company.

Monsoon Wedding (2002)
A stressed father, a bride-to-be with a secret, a smitten event planner, and relatives from around the world create much ado about the preparations for an arranged marriage in India.

North Country (2005)
A fictionalized account of the first major successful sexual harassment case in the United States—*Jenson vs. Eveleth Mines*, where a woman who

of jobs from industrialized First World countries to locations where labor is cheap has continued. According to the garment workers' union, UNITE HERE, so many textile-related jobs have been transferred to Third World countries that the union has only about 3,000 members left here in the United States.

endured a range of abuse while working as a miner filed and won the landmark 1984 lawsuit.

A Raisin in the Sun (1961; 2008)
An African-American family struggles with poverty, racism, and inner conflict as they strive for a better way of life. Based on the play by Lorraine Hansberry.

Salaam Bombay (1988)
The story of Krishna, Manju, Chillum and the other children on the streets of Bombay. Sometimes they can get a temporary job selling tea, but mostly they have to beg for money and keep out of the way of the police.

Silkwood (1983)
The story of Karen Silkwood, a metallurgy worker at a plutonium processing plant who was purposefully contaminated, psychologically tortured and possibly murdered to prevent her from exposing blatant worker safety violations at the plant.

Slumdog Millionaire (2008)
A Mumbai teen who grew up in the slums, becomes a contestant on the Indian version of "Who Wants To Be A Millionaire?" He is arrested under suspicion of cheating, and while being interrogated, events from his life history are shown which explain why he knows the answers.

To Kill a Mockingbird (1962)
Atticus Finch, a lawyer in the Depression-era South, defends a black man against an undeserved rape charge, and his kids against prejudice.

V for Vendetta (2006)
A shadowy freedom fighter known only as "V" uses terrorist tactics to fight against his totalitarian society.

Whale Rider (2002)
A contemporary story of love, rejection and triumph as a young Maori girl fights to fulfill a destiny her grandfather refuses to recognize.

Working Girl (1988)
When a secretary's idea is stolen by her boss, she seizes an opportunity to steal it back by pretending she has her boss's job.

*All synopses provided by the Internet Movie Database (IMDB): http://www.imdb.com/

(For comparison's sake, consider that the peak membership for the needlework trades union was 450,000 in 1969.) Resistance to and protest against exploitation of workers in less developed countries and to job exportation in the First World has not been translated into legal victories or meaningful social change to eliminate sweatshops or to stop the steady leakage of jobs from industrialized nations to places like Bangladesh and Haiti.

Resistance Within Developing Countries

Resistance to social inequalities brought about by globalization has not been limited to the developed world. There is also resistance from the "bottom up," that is, resistance by people in the developing world to the unequal conditions thrust upon them by globalizing industries. As these people—women, factory workers, farmers—begin to create a shared vision, what emerges is a phenomenon that historian Jeremy Brecher has called **globalization from below**. Indeed, alliances of economically disenfranchised people, based on shared ideas and cross-border cooperation, have achieved victories. According to Ferus-Comelo, for example, hundreds of young Korean women in a South Korean electronics plant occupied their factory for weeks when the company threatened to relocate. Similarly, workers on strike in Bangalore, India, lay down in front of trucks attempting to bring replacement workers into factories.

Perhaps one of the most significant victories for Third World resistance happened in Cochabamba, Bolivia. The Bolivian government had caved in to pressure from global financial institutions, such as the World Bank, and had sold off the water supply of Cochabamba (the country's third largest city) to Bechtel, a San Francisco-based company. The people of Cochabamba responded with strong protests, general strikes, and street blockades, effectively shutting down the town. Ultimately, the government gave in to protesters' demands and asked Bechtel to leave Bolivia. Not only did the people of Cochabamba regain control over their water supply, but indigenous peoples around the globe saw that it was possible to say "no" to unjust practices associated with globalization. Brecher has attributed victories like the one in Cochabamba to something he calls the **Lilliput Strategy**, a concept derived from a novel penned by Jonathan Swift in 1726. The novel describes an encounter between an Englishman of average build by human standards and a group of tiny people called Lilliputians who manage to subdue this "giant" by joining forces and working together. In like manner, Brecher's Lilliput Strategy involves organizing and maintaining grassroots solidarity among peoples experiencing the brunt of globalization.

Unfortunately, for every victory, there are many defeats. As the gap of inequality between rich and poor grows wider, some people wonder if the problems that have emerged from this imbalance can be resolved through demonstrations and protests. This question has created a new antiglobalization dynamic that focuses on dialogue rather than confrontation. In 2001, a group of opponents of global inequality came up with an idea that they hoped would encourage more Third World and grassroots participation in the debate over globalization. The **World Social Forum (WSF)**, as this movement was called, issued a charter of principles, key among which were economic justice, democracy, environmental protection, human rights, and national sovereignty. The movement took as its motto "Another World is Possible," and WSF leadership proceeded to organize biannual global conferences that provided a meeting place for individuals who opposed globalization but sought to express that opposition through discourse rather than strikes and street protests. The WSF held its first meeting in 2001 in Brazil. Subsequent meetings have been held in India, Pakistan, Venezuela, and Kenya. WSF meetings provide a forum-like setting where representatives of nongovernmental organizations from many nations can strategize about the inequalities brought about by globalization. Some WSF meetings have drawn as many as 75,000 delegates.

EFFORTS TO FIGHT INEQUALITY AND OPPRESSION WITHIN THE UNITED STATES
Policy and Law

One of the most effective, though perhaps not popular, ways to fight inequality and oppression is by enacting legislation that explicitly deals with the more harmful consequences of stratification and inequality. Of course, it is impossible to forcibly legislate *attitudes*—people are always free to think and believe what they will—but many scholars believe that attitudes and values follow changes at the macro level. For example, in the 1950s and '60s, most white Americans vehemently opposed school desegregation, the practice of integrating blacks into white schools and vice versa. In fact, Alabama Governor George Wallace physically blocked black students from entering the University of Alabama and moved only after being confronted by the National Guard. Other state officials took similar positions. Senator Harry Byrd closed schools in Virginia rather than desegregate them, and Orval Faubus, the governor of Arkansas, ordered the state's National Guard to block black students (now referred to as the "Little Rock Nine") from entering a high school in Little Rock. Over time, however, the attitudes of most white Americans changed when they realized they had nothing to fear from black students attending the same schools as their children and nothing to lose from impeding desegregation.

Beyond the issue of school desegregation, there have been numerous policies and laws passed over the last few decades that have helped reduce inequalities based on gender, race, income, sexual orientation, and other characteristics. As noted in an earlier chapter, inequalities based on age and species are widely accepted; consequently, we have witnessed fewer policy changes geared toward children and animals than toward other groups. In fact, when children are considered, the focus is often connected to parental *income inequality*, for example,

School Desegregation: The Sylvia Mendez Story

Most of us have the impression that school desegregation resulted from *Brown v. Board of Education* in 1954 and the resulting U.S. Supreme Court decision that separate public schools for blacks and whites were unconstitutional. What many people don't realize is that school segregation was already being challenged in various states.

At age 8, Sylvia Mendez was the center of a major case involving school desegregation. In 1946, she had been denied admission to an all-white school in Los Angeles, California, and told to enroll in a school for Mexican-American children. Her parents (along with 4 other families) sued and won their case. Mendez became "the first Hispanic student at an all-white school in California." In 2010, she was awarded the Presidential Medal of Freedom—the highest honor bestowed upon civilians in recognition of their contributions to the national interest.

Source: http://neatoday.org/2011/02/16/sylvia-mendez-school-desegregation-pioneer-honored-at-white-house/

the CHIP (Children's Health Insurance Program) that provides health insurance for uninsured children under age 19 who are not eligible for Medicaid. In the case of animals, the greatest response is prompted by concerns about food safety for humans (for example, the furor over Mad Cow Disease). Ironically, Congress has yet to pass a bill requiring that **downed cows** (those too sick to walk or stand) be euthanatized to ensure that they do not enter the human food chain. The lack of legislation and policy directed at protecting children and animals is likely a reflection of their relative status in society.

In contrast, there has been powerful legislation regarding race, gender, social class, and increasingly, sexual orientation. We turn now to just a few examples of laws and policies that have shaped people's lives over the past several decades.

Affirmative Action

Since the 1960s, affirmative action policies have sought to provide equal opportunities to groups that have been traditionally discriminated against, including racial minorities and women. Affirmative action provides guidelines for hiring and training for employers in the public sector (state or federal) and those who contract with the government and receive at least $50,000 in government monies and employ at least 50 workers. It also applies to educational institutions that use public funds (thus, many private schools are exempt). For instance, the law requires that organizations advertise jobs where minorities are likely to see the notices.

Affirmative action is one of the most important, and most misunderstood, of all government policies. To clarify one misconception, affirmative action does not mean that minorities or women will be hired regardless of their qualifications. If two candidates apply for a job, and one is a racial minority, then preference may be given to that candidate on the basis of membership to one of the protected groups—but only if the two applicants are *equally qualified* for the job. Affirmative action programs do not support the hiring of unqualified people. In fact, such practices are prohibited by law. Affirmative action was instituted to enable competent and qualified women and racial minorities to compete for employment in areas where they have been traditionally underrepresented. Contrary to another prevalent belief, affirmative action programs do not employ quotas. Employers may set flexible goals for ensuring a diverse workplace, but quotas are illegal.

Affirmative Action and College Admissions

For years, major public colleges and universities in the United States have taken race, ethnicity, and gender into account when making decisions about admitting first-year students. That is, in an effort to increase diversity, universities and colleges use race, ethnicity or sex as just a few of the many factors considered when deciding whether to admit a student. Such policies were criticized and contested by those who saw them as preferential treatment for minorities, one that lowered the chances of members of other groups (mostly white men) from being admitted to the best schools. Responding to the latter view, in 1996 California adopted Proposition 209, which prohibited public institutions from using race, sex, or ethnicity as a factor in admission decisions. Not long after, a Texas court ruled that such practices were unconstitutional. In 1999, Florida followed suit.

What effect did this change have on college admissions? David Colburn and his associates researched this issue by comparing first-year enrollments in California, Texas, and Florida before and after these changes in policy. What they found was quite interesting. The hardest hit group was African Americans. For instance, in California, the percentage of blacks entering the 3 most competitive universities was 6.51 percent in 1995; by 2005, just 2.97 percent entered. Black males were especially hard hit. At UC San Diego, only .51 percent of the first year students admitted in 2005 were black men. Enrollments for Hispanics also declined. Enrollment for Asians increased. What about white enrollment? Colburn, et al. found that white enrollment at the five major universities in California, Texas, and Florida actually *declined*. They acknowledge that this may have been due (in part) to the shrinking proportion of whites in these states but also noted: "For those who campaigned for the elimination of affirmative action in the belief that it would advantage the admission of white students, the trend over the past eight years can hardly be satisfying."

Title IX

Sport has traditionally been framed as a domain of masculinity. Young women and girls played sports in the past, of course, but they were more than likely told that women's sport is for fitness and socializing, not competition. In 1972, that changed with the passage of Title IX, which requires gender equity in sports participation in all educational institutions that receive government funding. Without a doubt, Title IX has had a profound effect on girls' and women's sports. In 1971 (the year before passage of the law), 3.67 million boys played interscholastic high school sports but only 294,015 girls did, a ratio of more than 12:1. Between 1972 and 2008, boys' participation rates increased to 4.2 million, while girls' participation rates skyrocketed to 2.95 million. The current ratio of female to male athletes is now 7:5—still a bit imbalanced but a far cry from 12:1. In retrospect it is easy to see that women and girls were not disinterested in sports; rather, they simply lacked the opportunity to participate, compete, and earn athletic scholarships via sports.

Social Security and Welfare Programs

Significant policies have been enacted to assist individuals who are most affected by economic inequality. **Welfare**, as we know it, began in the 1930s following the collapse of the U.S. economy during the Great Depression. "Welfare" is actually a patchwork of different social programs aimed to assist unemployed workers and their dependents and includes such things as food stamps, rent assistance, and marriage encouragement. **Social Security**, which was created in 1935, provides income to the elderly and stop-gap compensation for the unemployed. Assistance to lower-income, single-parent families was provided through a program known as **Aid to Families with Dependent Children** (AFDC).

In 1996, welfare programs were overhauled. With the passage of the Personal Responsibility and Work Opportunity Act of 1996, limitations on the duration and types of assistance that people could obtain were implemented. For instance, there is now a five-year lifetime limit on cash assistance, and recipients must work within two years. These limitations on assistance, and the recent economic downturn, have served to worsen the lives of the poorest Americans.

Same-Sex Marriage Laws

Until a few decades ago, heterosexual marriage was a "given." That changed when same-sex couples and other advocates challenged marriage laws, claiming them to be discriminatory. In response, the United States Congress overwhelmingly approved the federal **Defense of Marriage Act** (DOMA) in 1996. The purpose of this act was to define marriage as a union between a man and a woman, making it illegal for same-sex couples to marry. As of 2011, 29 states also had constitutional amendments restricting marriage to one man and one woman.

At present, six states (Massachusetts, Connecticut, Iowa, New Hampshire, Vermont, and New York) as well as the District of Columbia, grant marriage certificates to same-sex couples. One other state, Maryland, recognize same-sex marriages that were legally entered into in other jurisdictions, and twelve other states offer at least some state-level spousal benefits. In early 2011, the Obama administration vowed that it will no longer defend the Defense of Marriage Act.

Violence Against Women Act (VAWA)

Although American society had come to understand and define violence against women as a social problem worthy of immediate attention, our laws, public policies, and judicial practices were not in line with combating this problem. In 1994, the **Violence Against Women Act** was passed; as a result, much more attention and resources are paid to gender violence. The VAWA provides protection and services to women who are victims of violence, including domestic violence and intimate partner violence, as well as dating violence, sexual assault, and stalking. Since the mid-1990s, the focus of VAWA has shifted from one of reactivity to one of proactivity. Rather than providing assistance to victims, programs and services with the sole intent of preventing violence against women, education of the general public about the personal and societal harms of such violence are now being initiated.

Community Activism

We should point out that many of the legislative changes discussed above were the result of **social movements**. Social movements refer to collective action taken by organized groups who lack institutionalized power and seek to effect change. The changes in employment practices, for example, resulted in large part from the Civil Rights Movement. The Women's Movement was responsible for making violence against women, including sexual harassment, a crime and raising the public's awareness of domestic violence. We see gay-rights activists and other advocates working collectively now to change marriage laws throughout the country, and these individuals have been instrumental in including violence against gays and lesbians in hate crime legislation. These groups remind us of historian Howard Zinn's wise words from *A People's History of the United States*: "We don't have to engage in grand, heroic actions to participate in the process of change. Small acts, when multiplied by millions of people, can transform the world."

But social change can also occur on local levels. Take, for example, the efforts of Hamilton County residents (where Cincinnati, Ohio, is located) to create and sustain intentional communities that are racially and economically integrated. Whereas most communities in the United States remain segregated by race and social class, Cincinnati neighborhoods have achieved greater diversity. Residents report many benefits, including learning about others who are different from themselves, having safer communities, and a greater engagement in community events and democratic decision making. Importantly, the Cincinnatus Association reports that integration did not lower the socioeconomic status of neighborhoods, nor did it produce predominantly black neighborhoods (which often occurs when whites move out of neighborhoods that are becoming racially integrated—a process referred to as "white flight").

Another example of community activism, in this case involving local businesses, can be found in the "pay what you can afford" movement. Across the country, restaurants allow customers to pay whatever they can afford to. Business owners report that their businesses have actually improved after they implemented this system.

We can also find examples of cities and towns joining forces to ban activities that promote violence against various groups. For example, Albuquerque, New Mexico, and South Lake Tahoe, California, have banned the sale of dogs and cats in retail stores, after recognizing that many of these animals were bred in puppy mills and by cat breeders under cruel and unhealthy conditions. Individuals in New York City banded together to urge a popular club from hosting fascist bands. Each year, thousands of women across the country (and worldwide) take part in the Take Back the Night gatherings, often marching in solidarity down city streets, to raise awareness of violence against women. The list goes on and on. Chances are there are groups in your own area working to end discrimination of various kinds.

Personal Change

Ultimately, all social change starts at the individual level, with the decisions and choices you make. For many of us, however, it can be overwhelming to think about taking a stand and making a change, even when it's regarding something about which we feel strongly. There are reasons for this reluctance. There is the tendency for individuals to be "free riders"—to enjoy the benefits others have fought for but not contribute to the effort. Social psychologists have also identified the "diffusion of responsibility" phenomenon, whereby we expect others around us to take action and hence do nothing ourselves.

One of the most challenging barriers to social change is the increased distance that lies between people in contemporary society. Distance formed by new technologies and other social barriers can lead to what sociologist D. Stanley Eitzen calls **social atrophy**. So much of our social interaction now occurs in virtual environments: on Facebook, in Web-based college courses, via Twitter. Without face-to-face interaction it is harder to combat stereotypes, challenge prejudice, and learn how to live among an increasingly diverse population.

But throughout history, individuals—whether acting alone and or in groups—have changed the world. Consider Harvey Milk, Norma Rae, Rosa Parks, Narayanan Krishnan, Erin Brockovich, Robert Gould Shaw, Oskar Schindler, Wesley Autrey, Rev. Martin L. King, Jr., Josie Aimes, Tanya McCloskey, Marcia Kadish, and thousands others. If any of these names are unfamiliar, research their stories. Their actions can inspire us all to treat others fairly and to be a force for change.

Sometimes it starts with a simple shift in perspective. Indeed, the value of the sociological perspective is to help us step outside of our own perspective and see that many of the assumptions we make about others are based upon limited knowledge and stereotyping. It means recognizing ways in which you are privileged—not from anything you've done to earn it but simply from a physical attribute such as skin color or sex, or from birth location (nationality, family). You cannot necessarily lose or refuse your privilege, but you can use your privilege for good. Once you see that even those who are privileged suffer, in direct and indirect ways, it may be easier to fight for change.

It may also help to remember a fundamental fact about stratification that we discussed in this volume—that stratification systems intersect in myriad ways. By implication, fighting injustice toward one group will help other groups. So which "cause" you focus on may be less important than simply doing something.

SUMMARY
This concluding chapter comprised just a few examples of efforts that are working to bring balance to society in terms of gender, race, class, species, and the environment. There is still a great deal of work that needs doing, so this chapter really serves as a beginning rather than an end. Whether stratification and inequality can be mitigated by us "little people" is a question that cannot yet be answered. But one thing is clear: The future is in the hands of readers like you, whose choices, decisions, and strategies will help determine the future of our globalizing planet.

Further Reading

Ehrenreich, Barbara. *Nickel and Dimed: On (Not) Getting By in America*. New York: Henry Holt & Company, 2008.

Hays, Sharon. *Flat Broke with Children: Women in the Age of Welfare Reform*. New York; Oxford: Oxford University Press, 2004.

Naples, Nancy A., and Desai, Manisha, eds. *Women's Activism and Globalization: Linking Local Struggles and Transnational Politics*. New York: Routledge, 2002.

Zinn, Howard. *The Twentieth Century*. London: Harper Perennial, 2003.

Zinn, Howard. *A People's History of the United States 1492 to Present*. London: Harper Perennial Modern Classics, 2009.

GLOSSARY

accomplishment of natural growth   A parenting style most often utilized by poor or working-class families in which parents are more likely to let children develop "naturally" with limited parental supervision.

achieved characteristics   Characteristics acquired or earned through concerted effort (include marital status, education, occupation, etc.).

affirmative action   Antidiscrimination policies directed at correcting inequality on the basis of race and sex through programs designed to encourage businesses and schools to recruit qualified minorities and women.

ageism   Discrimination on the basis of age; typically involves prejudice against very young segments of the population or the elderly.

Aid to Families with Dependent Children (AFDC)   A federal assistance program aimed at providing income to children who come from families with little to no income; AFDC was replaced by Temporary Assistance for Needy Families (TANF) in 1996.

alleles   Gene variants that tend to be associated more with one group than another.

all-weather bigot   An individual who is both prejudiced and discriminatory.

all-weather liberal   An individual who is neither prejudiced nor discriminatory.

anatomy   Physical elements of the human body (i.e., penis, vagina, breasts); governs reproduction and sexual interactions.

androgyny   A state of appearing or presenting oneself as neither feminine nor masculine.

anthropocentric   A view that focuses exclusively on humans; regards human values and experiences as central to the universe.

anthropomorphism   The process of attributing human characteristics (emotions, motivations, or behaviors) to animals.

antiglobalization movement   A social and political movement that is critical of corporate capitalism and its effect on growing disparity among the international community.

antimiscegenation laws   Laws that prohibited interracial marriage; originally intended to prevent intermarriage between blacks and whites.

ascribed characteristics   Characteristics with which you are born (race, sex, height, eye color, etc.).

asymmetry in cultural evaluations of gender   The recognition that women everywhere lack generally recognized and culturally valued authority; that is, women are valued less than men, even if they perform the same role as men.

bourgeoisie   In Marxian conflict theory, this is the elite class of people who owned property, factories, and production processes; exploiters of the proletariat.

capital   Access to tangible resources in society (money, services, opportunity, etc.)

capitalism   The economic system in which the "means of production" (the "stuff" from which materials are produced) are owned by a few individuals; the labor is provided by other people, many of whom cannot afford the products they help create.

care deficit   A deficit in child care and domestic work caused by the increasing number of women in the workforce and the decreasing number of social services available for children and families; creates a deficit that is filled by nannies and domestics from developing nations.

caste system   A closed system of stratification in which heredity determines one's place in society, and movement between classes is not possible.

chattel   A tangible, moveable form of property other than land.

collective dislocation   The process through which large numbers of people move to escape natural disasters or wars, are forced to leave an area because of development projects, or move to seek employment opportunities.

colonization   The process of a developed nation sending people (colonists) to establish a settlement in order to establish markets in new areas of the globe; enables the colonizer to extract goods (rubber, copper, gold) or services (cheap labor) from the colonized country.

color-blind racism   A form of modern racism which explains contemporary racial inequality as the outcome of nonracial dynamics; commonly associated with the belief that race (color) is no longer an effective concept for explaining racial disparities.

concentrated animal feeding operations (CAFOs)   Agricultural operations in which animals are confined in large numbers without grass, sunshine, or vegetation, as opposed to being allowed to roam freely and graze.

concerted cultivation   A parenting style most often utilized by middle-class families in which parents seek to "cultivate" their children's talents and interests in a "concerted" or purposeful fashion.

consumption model   A social model in which individuals and families earn a wage and then utilize that money to purchase needed resources.

coverture   A common law practice stipulating that women become the property of men upon entering into a marriage contract.

cultural ideology   Widespread beliefs about the rightness of certain cultural practices which are used to justify keeping a practice or system in place.

de facto segregation   Segregation in practice or in reality; racial separation which appears to result from voluntary choices, but is actually caused by structural inequalities.

de jure segregation   Segregation by law; commonly associated with Jim Crow segregation that was based on the principle of "separate but equal" (1890s–1960s).

Defense of Marriage Act (DOMA)   A 1996 act designed to define marriage as a union between a man and a woman, making it illegal for same-sex couples to marry.

diffusion of responsibility   The reduction of responsibility for taking action because others are already taking action; people's willingness to do something diminishes as the size of the active group increases.

discrimination   Behavior that results in unfair treatment of a person or group on the basis of group membership.

Divine Right of Kings   A religious doctrine stating that monarchs derive their authority directly from God and therefore have the right to command others.

doing gender   The day-to-day process through which we continually display and accomplish our gender through social interaction.

domestic violence (DV)   Violence directed at members of one's own household; most commonly refers to assaults committed against women by their male partners.

double stigmatization   A term used to explain the circumstances faced by African American men who have criminal records and must contend both with racial prejudice and with the social burden associated with having a criminal record.

downed cows   Cows too sick to walk or stand; the word "downed" can be used to describe like circumstances in other animals as well.

downward mobility   A decline in social standing, often the result of job loss, divorce, demotion, or widespread stock-market downturns.

egalitarianism   The idea that everyone is an equal partner; in terms of gender, it is the idea that men and women should be equal in relationships (duties, responsibilities, etc.).

ethnicity   Refers to groups that are defined primarily by aspects of cultural heritage or identity (e.g., food, clothing, language).

fair-weather liberals   Individuals who are not prejudiced, but whose actions discriminate nonetheless.

fatherhood bonus/ motherhood penalty   The social outcome whereby men benefit from parenthood by earning more while women do not.

female genital cutting (FGC)   A procedure in which female genital organs are intentionally altered for nonmedical purposes (typically involving whole or partial removal of external genitalia; particularly the labia or clitoris).

feminization of migration   The phenomena characterized by the overwhelming number of young women who become production workers in multinational corporations. Many of these women move from their country of origin for the specific purpose of working.

feudalism   A system of stratification based on heredity; large numbers of peasants, serfs and laborers worked for and lived beneath a handful of aristocratic landowners.

gender   Cultural ideas and expectations associated with persons of different sexes; society's relative definition of men and women (masculinity and femininity).

gendered organizations   Organizations with norms and practices based on masculine norms and practices; such practices are visible in division of labor, allowed behaviors, physical spaces, and so on.

gendered play   The pleasure or joy derived from being recognized for fulfilling certain social expectations associated with your gender.

General Agreement on Tariffs and Trades (GATT)   Formed in 1947 and replaced by WTO in 1995, this agreement sought to regulate world trade following World War II.

Global South A term used to refer to those parts of the world that have greatly suffered from the effects of globalization.

globalization The process through which the lives of human beings living in very different parts of the globe become more and more interconnected.

globalization from below Resistance by people in the developing world to the unequal conditions thrust upon them by globalizing industries; resistance from the "bottom up."

hierarchy The categorization of groups of people by rank order; certain groups are perceived to be above others.

human trafficking The sale and transport of human beings for profit; human beings are forced to provide labor or services for others.

hypodescent rule The practice of classifying mixed-race persons as members of the more socially subordinate or "inferior" race of those that comprise their genetic heredity.

ideological racism Widespread, societal-level beliefs about the perceived inferiority of certain racial groups.

ideologies Widespread cultural beliefs or collection of ideas that reflect social wants, needs, and desires.

infant mortality The number of babies who die at birth or during the first year of life (measured as a rate: deaths per 1,000 live births).

infanticide The killing of an infant, typically by a parent or family member.

institutional discrimination Unequal (and detrimental) treatment of an entire group, which is practiced within social institutions (education, housing, economy, etc.).

interlocking directorates The linkages among corporations that are formed by individuals who sit on multiple corporate boards.

intersex Individuals who do not fit clearly within the medical community's definition of either male or female; characterized by "medically ambiguous" genitalia.

intimate partner violence (IPV) Physical, sexual, or psychological damage by a current or former partner; includes people who do not share a domicile and people who are not sexually intimate.

Last-In First-Out (LIFO) An employment practice in which the most recently hired people are the first employees let go in the case of corporate difficulties or restructuring.

life expectancy The average number of years one can expect to live depending on a variety of biological and social conditions; average expected age at death.

Lilliput Strategy   A term coined by Jeremy Brecher, this refers to a form of organizing and maintaining grassroots solidarity among peoples experiencing the brunt of globalization.

living wage   The amount of money individuals must earn in order to support themselves and their families; this figure is substantially higher than our current minimum wage.

maquiladoras   Factories along the U.S.–Mexico border where workers assemble products for export that have actually been imported solely for the purpose of re-export; these factories are a direct off-shoot of globalization and are supported by NAFTA.

melanin   The pigment found in skin, which determines skin color.

meritocracy   A system based in the belief that personal and professional successes are based on achievement and merit earned through hard work alone.

minimum wage   A federal and/or state mandated hourly minimum for how much an employee must be paid on a given job.

morbidity   The incidence of illness within a given population.

mortality   Deaths in a population; often conveyed as a ratio (deaths per 100,000 population).

motherhood penalty   See fatherhood bonus.

multinational corporations   Large corporations that have production, manufacturing, and marketing components in multiple countries; poorer nations often serve as the source of production for a particular product that is then marketed in other, richer nations.

neoteny   The condition of retaining youthful, childlike features in adult forms (both human and animal).

North American Free Trade Agreement (NAFTA)   A trade agreement signed by the nations of Canada, Mexico, and the United States; the intent of this agreement is free trade among these nations, but it has resulted in the exploitation of certain workforces.

one drop rule   A legal standard which stated that "one drop" of black blood meant that someone was considered legally black.

open-class system   A system of stratification that allows for movement between classes; individuals have the ability to improve or worsen their social standing.

oppression   Extreme exercise of authority or power over others; a state of being surrounded by a network of barriers and pressures that shape all aspects of one's life.

opt-out revolution   A recent trend among women who, after achieving high-powered careers, are opting out of the workforce to care for their children and homes.

othering   A phenomenon that occurs when individuals in power are perceived as the "normal" and desirable group, and individuals who do not fall within that group are perceived as different, "less than," and inferior.

outsourcing   The practice of contracting (to workers in developing countries) much of the service work that was once performed in a developed nation.

phenotypes   Observable physical characteristics such as hair color, skin color, shape of eyes, and distinct facial features.

polite racism   A "modern" form of racism practiced by those who harbor racially prejudiced beliefs but understand that blatantly and overtly sharing such attitudes is socially unacceptable.

power elite   A small and very close group at the top who wield extraordinary power and possess extraordinary wealth.

prejudice   Unfavorable opinions, feelings, or judgments about a group of people on the basis of a particular characteristic; a prejudgment or belief in the inferiority of a group.

premature mortality   Deaths occurring in the United States before age 75.

prestige   The honor and esteem associated with holding a certain position or place within the social hierarchy.

privilege   Unearned advantage that people may experience regardless of merit or achievement; privilege is typically enjoyed by those in the most advantageous position relative to any particular form of stratification.

proletariat   In Marxian theory, this refers to working-class people who had nothing to offer but their labor, which supported the financial riches of the bourgeoisie.

race   A social construct that refers to a group of people who share some sort of outwardly defining physical characteristics; racial classifications typically rely on continental groupings.

racial prejudice   Unfavorable opinions, feelings, or judgments about a particular racial group; belief in the inferiority of a racial group.

racial profiling   The practice of police singling out of members of racial or ethnic minority groups for questioning or interrogation, based upon nothing or little more than their race/ethnicity.

racial stereotypes   Exaggerated and oversimplified beliefs about members of a particular racial group.

second shift   The gender gap in labor within the home that reflects an abundance of domestic work completed by women upon returning home from a day in the workplace; that is, women have two full-time jobs.

separate spheres   The separation between work and home that began in the late 1700s with the Industrial Revolution; it represents a cultural belief that women are responsible for the home, while men are responsible for earning a wage.

sex   Biological and anatomical characters that are associated with reproductive and sexual activity.

sex chromosomes   Genetically encoded information that determine physical and sexual development (XX for female, XY for male).

sex hormones   Chemicals in the body (estrogen, testosterone, progesterone) that play an important role in sexual development (puberty) and reproduction.

sex slavery   Sexual exploitation in which individuals are sold, transported, and forced to perform sexual services, oftentimes in addition to performing other forms of labor.

sexual harassment   Unwelcome sexual advances, requests for sexual favors, and other verbal or physical conduct of a sexual nature.

slavery   A system of economic stratification based upon ownership of certain groups of people; slaves are considered to be and are treated as property and can be sold and bought.

social atrophy   Social isolation due to the distance formed by new technologies and other social barriers.

social constructions   Any institution, characteristic, or concept whose meaning or significance is created through social, historical, and political processes.

social mobility   The movement between classes that is possible in open-class systems.

social movements   Collective action taken by organized groups who lack institutionalized power and seek to effect change.

social problem   A culturally defined social condition or issue that negatively affects the proper functioning of society.

Social Security   A social program that provides income to elderly persons and various other people who meet the criteria for supplemental income and aid.

socioeconomic status (SES)   A combination of social and economic indicators that determine an individual's status; often measured by income, education, and occupational status; SES may also include prestige, power, and respect.

speciesism   Belief in the inherent superiority of humans over other animals; intolerance of and discrimination against animals by humans, often through cruelty and exploitation.

stereotype   An exaggerated and often oversimplified belief associated with a particular group of people.

stratification   The division of society according to certain social categories such as race, class, and gender; the system by which societies organize themselves and determine the distribution of scarce resources.

sweatshop factories   Workplaces that subject workers to extreme economic exploitation and often physical abuse for miniscule wages.

systemic   Having the characteristic of being built into the very fabric of society—its norms, institutions, values, laws, and so on.

third shift   The additional labor of worrying about the children, the home, work, and all the other demands on women's busy lives (comes after professional and domestic work).

timid bigot   An individual who is prejudiced but does not discriminate.

Trail of Tears   The relocation of thousands of Cherokee from their lands to "Indian Territory" during which thousands died and those who resisted being relocated were forcibly removed or killed; culminated in the Indian Removal Act of 1830 which stated that all Native Americans living east of the Mississippi River were to be forced onto reservation land west of the Mississippi.

transgender   A blanket term used to describe the incongruence between the embodiment and display of gender with one's biological sex according to contemporary standards.

Tuskegee syphilis experiment   40-year-long government medical experiment (1932–1972) in which the U.S. Public Health Service studied syphilis among 399 poor African American men in Tuskegee, Alabama. Researchers failed to treat patients and withheld information about the disease even after it became known that penicillin was effective in treating syphilis.

upward mobility   The process of improving one's social standing.

vegans   Individuals who do not eat eggs, dairy products, or anything else that is derived from or created with the help of animal byproducts.

vegetarians   People who eat no meat, including fish, beef or poultry; people may choose to practice vegetarianism in varying degrees.

Violence Against Women Act (VAWA)   1994 federal law that provides protection and services to women who are victims of violence (includes domestic violence, intimate partner violence, dating violence, sexual assault, and stalking).

wealth   The accumulation of money or assets in excess of someone's expenses; this excess can be passed on to future generations.

welfare   A patchwork of different social programs aimed at assisting unemployed workers and their dependents and intended to make people self-sufficient.

white privilege   Refers to advantages associated with being white in contemporary society; unseen privilege which places white people in an advantageous position.

white supremacy   System in which whites are perceived as superior to other racial groups and thereby retain power and control.

working poor   People who work but nevertheless fall under the poverty line, or work and earn an income above the official poverty line but are still unable to cover their living expenses.

World Social Forum (WSF)   An organization dedicated to increasing dialog about globalization and creating partnerships between First World and Third World citizens.

World Trade Organization (WTO)   An international agency that encourages trade between 153 member nations, administers global trade agreements, and resolves trade disputes.

BIBLIOGRAPHY

Acker, Joan. "Hierarchies, jobs, bodies: A theory of gendered organizations" *Gender & Society* 4 (1990): 139-158.

Ariès, Philippe. *Centuries of Childhood.* London: Pimlico, 1996.

Ascione, Frank R., and Phil Arkow. *Child Abuse, Domestic Violence, and Animal Abuse: Linking the Circles of Compassion for Prevention and Intervention.* West Lafayette, Ind: Purdue University Press, 1999.

Atwood-Harvey, Dana. "From touchstone to tombstone: Children's experiences with the abuse of their beloved pets." *Humanity & Society* 31 (2007): 379-400.

Bertrand, Marianne and Sendhil Mullainathan. "Are Emily and Greg More Employable than Lakisha and Jamal? A Field Experiment on Labor Market Discrimination." *The American Economic Review* 94 (2004): 991-1013.

Bolton, Michele. *The Third Shift: Managing Hard Choices in Our Careers, Homes, and Lives as Women.* San Francisco: Jossey-Bass, 2000.

Bonilla-Silva, Eduardo. *Racism Without Racists: Color-blind Racism and the Persistence of Racial Inequality in the United States.* Lanham: Rowman & Littlefield Publishers, 2006.

Brecher, Jeremy, Tim Costello, and Brendan Smith. *Globalization from Below.* Boston: South End Press, 2000.

Chang, Leslie T. *Factory Girls: From Village to City in a Changing China.* New York: Spiegel and Grau, 2009.

Colburn, David R. "Admissions and Public Higher education in California, Texas, and Florida: The Post-Affirmative Action Era" *InterActions: UCLA Journal of Education and Information Studies* 4(1) 1-21, 2008.

Corsaro, William. *The Sociology of Childhood*. Thousand Oaks, Calif.: Pine Forge Press, 1997.

Crawley, Sara L., Lara J. Foley, and Constance L. Shehan. *Gendering Bodies*. Lanham: Rowman & Littlefield Publishers, 2008.

Domhoff, G. William. *Who Rules America? Power and Politics and Social Change*. Boston, Mass. [u.a.]: McGraw-Hill, 2006.

Ehrenreich, Barbara. *Nickel and Dimed: On (Not) Getting by in America*. New York: Henry Holt & Co, 2008.

Eitzen, D. Stanley, and Baca Zinn, Maxine. *Globalization: The Transformation of Social Worlds*. Belmont, Calif.: Wadsworth, 2009.

Ferus-Comelo, Anibel. "Double jeopardy: Gender and migration in electronics manufacturing." In *Challenging the Chip*, edited by Ted Smith, David A. Sonnenfield, and David Naguib, 42–54. Philadelphia: Temple University Press, 2006.

Fitzgerald, Amy J. "'They gave me a reason to live': The protective effects of companion animals on the suicidality of abused women." *Humanity & Society* 31 (2007): 355-378.

Frye, Marilyn. *The Politics of Reality*. Trumansburg, New York: The Crossing Press, 1983.

Gibson, Robert A. *The Negro Holocaust: Lynching and Race Riots in the United States, 1880–1950*. Yale-New Haven Teachers Institute, 1979.

Gilbert, Dennis L. *The American Class Structure in an Age of Growing Inequality*. Los Angeles: Pine Forge Press, 2011.

Grusky, David B. *Social Stratification: Class, Race, and Gender in Sociological Perspective*. Boulder, Colo.: Westview Press, 2001.

Harris, Daniel. *Cute, Quaint, Hungry, and Romantic: The Aesthetics of Consumerism*. New York: Da Capa Press, 2001.

Heymann, Jody. *The Widening Gap: Why America's Working Families Are in Jeopardy and What Can Be Done About It*. New York: Basic Books, 2000.

Hochschild, Arlie Russell, with Anne Machung. *The Second Shift*. New York: Avon Books, 1989.

Kimmel, Michael. *The Gendered Society*. 3rd ed. New York: Oxford University Press, 2008.

Lareau, Annette. 2007. *Unequal Childhoods: Class, Race, and Family Life*. Berkeley, CA: Univ. of California Press.

Maccoby, Eleanor Emmons, and Carol Nagy Jacklin. *The Psychology of Sex Differences*. Stanford, CA: Stanford Univ. Press, 1987.

Marcus, Erik. *Meat Market: Animals, Ethics, & Money.* Boston, Mass: Brio Press, 2005.

Massey, Douglas S. *Categorically Unequal: The American Stratification System.* New York: Russell Sage Foundation, 2007.

Melson, Gail F. *Why the Wild Things Are: Animals in the Lives of Children.* Cambridge, Mass.: Harvard University Press, 2001.

Parrenas, Rachel Salazar. "The care crisis in the Philippines: Children and transnational families in the new global economy," in *Global Woman: Nannies, Maids, and Sex Workers in the New Economy,* edited by Barbara Ehrenreich and Arlie Russell Hochschild, 39–54. New York: Henry Holt and Company, 2003.

Risman, Barbara J. *Gender Vertigo: American Families in Transition.* New Haven: Yale University Press, 1998.

Rothenberg, Paula S. *White Privilege: Essential Readings on the Other Side of Racism.* New York: Worth Publishers, 2005.

Schwalbe, Michael. *Rigging the Game: How Inequality Is Reproduced in Everyday Life.* New York: Oxford University Press, 2008.

Tilly, Charles. *Durable Inequality.* Berkeley, CA: University of California Press, 1999.

Valdez, Diana Washington. *The Killing Fields: Harvest of Women.* Austin: Peace at the Border Press, 2006.

Williams, Joan. *Unbending Gender: Why Family and Work Conflict and What to Do About It.* New York: Oxford Univ. Press, 2001.

Zinn, Howard. *A People's History of the United States 1492 to Present.* London: Harper Perennial Modern Classics, 2009.

INDEX

Index note: Page numbers followed by *g* indicate glossary entries.

A

abuse 83–86, 90
access to resources 8, 31
accomplishment of natural growth 29, 123*g*
achieved characteristics 6, 123*g*
Acker, Joan 64
activism 119–120
affirmative action 71, 116–117, 123*g*
ageism 76, 123*g*
Aid to Families with Dependent Children
   (AFDC) 118, 123*g*
alleles 36, 123*g*
all-weather bigot 12–13, 123*g*
all-weather liberal 12, 13, 123*g*
American Dream 26–27
anatomy 55, 123*g*
androgyny 72, 123*g*
animal feeding operations 84
animals 75–86, 90–92
   abuse of 83–86
   as companions 79–81
   cultural perceptions 76–79
   feeding operations 84, 125*g*
   oppression of 83
   sociological perspectives on 76
   status of 90–91

   as subordinates 81–83
   treatment of 76–79
anthropocentric 76, 124*g*
anthropomorphism 81, 124*g*
anti-globalization movement 111, 124*g*
antimisceganation laws 44, 124*g*
Aries, Philippe 86
ascribed characteristics 6, 124*g*
asymmetry in cultural evaluations of gender
   61–62, 124*g*
Atwood-Harvey, Dana 85
Ayres, Ian 28, 42

B

Baca Zinn, Maxine 103
Baker, David 31
Bechtel 114
Belkin, Lisa 58–59
Bertrand, Marianne 42
Best, Joel 88
Bianchi, Suzanne 67
bigotry 12–13
biological differences 5–6, 36–38, 55–61
Bolton, Michele 67
Bonilla-Silva, Eduardo 45